Small Stream Bass

Small Stream Bass

A Complete Angler's Guide to Bass Fishing Off the Beaten Path

TACKLE, TACTICS, TIMING, AND TRICKS

John Gifford

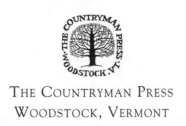

THE COUNTRYMAN PRESS
WOODSTOCK, VERMONT

Library of Congress Cataloging-in-Publication Data
Gifford, John Allen.
    Small stream bass : a complete angler's guide to bass fishing off the
    beaten path : tackle, tactics, timing, and tricks / John Gifford.
        p. cm.
    ISBN 0-88150-525-0
     1. Bass fishing. I. Title.
    SH681 .G54 2002
    799.1'773—dc21   2002074574

Book design by Faith Hague
Front cover photo © Barry & Cathy Beck
Illustrations © James J. DiStefano Jr., Fish Head Studio

Published by The Countryman Press
P.O. Box 748
Woodstock, Vermont 05091

Distributed by W.W. Norton & Company, Inc., 500 Fifth Avenue,
New York, NY 10110

Printed in the United States of America

10 9 8 7 6 5 4 3 2 1

For The Tootlebug:
I can't wait until we can fish
these streams together.

CONTENTS

8

ACKNOWLEDGMENTS

My pursuit of small-stream bass has been greatly facilitated and made more enjoyable as a result of the help of many people, all of whom deserve a hearty thank you, including: Ellen and Jackson, for their unwavering love, support, understanding, and for just being there; ditto for Mom and Dad, Foo, Pablo, and Jenn. I must thank Ellen and Eric Smith of St. Louis, Missouri, for their help and generosity, especially insofar as fly tying and photography are concerned. Thanks also to Tom and Terry Henneberry, Jay Armstrong, Tom Lunsford, and Russ and Mike Henneberry for their support, and to Karen and Gary at Tiffany's for their fine food and for always being there.

Thanks to Ed and Bob Story of Feather-Craft Fly Shop in St. Louis for their unparalleled wisdom and advice in all matters fly-tying.

I'd also like to thank the many private, state, and federal organizations—and their people—across the country who work to ensure that our small bass streams remain healthy and protected.

Finally, I'd like to express my appreciation to Kermit Hummel and the entire staff at The Countryman Press for their interest in this project.

INTRODUCTION

If you were to ask 100 people about the first image that comes to each of their minds upon hearing the phrase *bass fishing*, chances are the responses would be uniform and similar. Perhaps half would tell you that the image of a bass boat is the first thing that pops into their minds. Heavy casting tackle would likely rank highly, as would large lakes or reservoirs. And these responses wouldn't be unfounded.

But there is another aspect of fishing for black bass often ignored or overlooked by the general public, one even forsaken by most anglers. It takes place in venues you've likely driven over hundreds or thousands of times during your life: beneath nondescript bridges that unceremoniously bear the names of these virtually unknown destinations. And unless your earliest angling memories involve wading one of these minuscule waterways, chances are you've never even considered them worthy of your time.

Small streams flow through the countryside of every state in the union. They're found in all types of geography, from high mountains to plains to valleys and lowlands. What is important is that most of these streams support diverse aquatic life, and quite often they are home to surprising populations of black bass.

Notice that I said *bass*, not trout.

Trout are, in many ways, the quintessential stream fish. But largely because of their inability to tolerate warm water, they are limited in their geographic distribution. Of course, this is to say nothing of the many tailrace fisheries across the country, which have certainly enhanced the trout's appeal and availability as a sport fish. At any rate, trout are limited to cold-water habitats.

On the other hand, largemouth, smallmouth, and spotted bass may be found across the country, north to south, east to west. The optimal water temperatures for these creatures aren't too far removed from that of the trout, but it's their adaptability, heartiness, and resilience that help to account for their nationwide distribution. For example, an 80-degree water temperature might make a largemouth bass sluggish, perhaps sending the fish into a nocturnal feeding routine. However, such a water temperature approaches the lethal limit for rainbow and brown trout. It makes sense, then, that these fish should be considered worthy of your attention, especially because they're often found just outside your door.

But why the small streams?

If you've fished for any length of time, you've undoubtedly noticed that our lakes, reservoirs, and even many of our larger rivers are becoming more and more crowded. Fishing is an incredibly popular sport, attracting legions of new anglers each year. With the increasing number of anglers, the crowding of our favorite waters is inevitable. This phenomenon also translates to fewer opportunities for peace, solitude, and unmolested fish. This is where the small streams come in.

These overlooked creeks and streams, and their black bass, fill this void for the angler seeking a quality fishing experience. For as crowds continue to flock to the large waters, the quality experience is increasingly threatened.

If you're already well versed in small-stream fishing, then $\quad$
you probably realize that quality isn't derived solely from large
lakes, expensive bass boats, or even the opportunity of
catching big fish. Personally, I've had some of my most enjoyable days on small waters, regardless of the number of fish
caught. It was the ambiance that mattered—the scenery, the
tree-lined banks, and the seclusion. And as for the fish? Well,
tangling with wild, stream-run bass on light tackle makes
them all trophies.

On the other hand, if you've never experienced what it is
like to stand knee-deep in a cool, running stream at dawn,
alone, and casting to wild and wily bass, then you should find
this book enlightening. In this time of expensive fishing ex-
peditions, exotic destinations, and elaborate accommodations,
it is nice to know there are still some things money can't buy.

Whether you're new or experienced in this arena, it is my
hope that you'll find this book informative and useful. And in
the event that you aren't converted to a small-stream fanatic,
at the very least you'll discover a refreshing alternative to
those crowded larger waters.

I wish you good fishing.

John Gifford
Norman, Oklahoma
December 2001

Chapter 1

Small Water versus Large Water

A S IS THE CASE with most any angling endeavor, fishing small streams has its inherent rewards and drawbacks. Of course, opting to fish a lake or large river presents one with a very similar set of circumstances, both favorable and otherwise. It is a give-and-take situation. You can't have everything in any single case; rather, you must pick and choose the qualities most important to you.

Does the opportunity to fish all day without encountering another angler appeal to you? Or are you more concerned with catching truly large fish? If the latter, what are you willing to sacrifice in order to do so?

These are some of the questions you must ask yourself when choosing how to best spend your precious fishing time. But often the situation isn't so cut and dry. For example, fishing your favorite lake doesn't necessarily mean that you'll have to fight the crowds. And of course, you don't *have* to fish large water to catch large fish. Most small streams harbor secrets revealed only to those who take the time to get to know them. But in order to discover them, you'll have to forsake the large waters at times when you know that you can catch fish. You're ambivalent, I know. But let's explore our options.

Large lakes and reservoirs often entice anglers with their sheer numbers of fish. These waters, whether natural or constructed, support a diversity of aquatic life, encompassing everything from microscopic plankton to apex predators, such as largemouth bass. Because of their vast expanses and extensive, productive forage bases, large waters are usually able to sustain large quantities of predator fish. Of course, regular stockings by state and federal fish and wildlife departments certainly enhance this capability. And inevitably, many of these fish are able to grow to trophy proportions.

On the downside, large waters attract equally large crowds. For example, if the largemouth bass at a certain lake experience tremendous recruitment for a period of four or five years, thereby increasing their numbers exponentially, the word soon gets out that this lake is hot. The crowds, then, gravitate to the lake.

Similarly, when bass tournaments report exceptional results at the weigh-in table, both tournament and recreational anglers alike soon begin flocking to the lake in hopes of landing a trophy fish.

Large waters, then, are quick to divulge their secrets simply because they attract so many people. Obviously, the more hooks and lines you have in the water, the quicker these "secrets" are discovered, if there are any.

Of course, this is to say nothing of the pressure such crowds impose on the fish. This is how such techniques as "finesse fishing" arise; the more pressured the fish, the more elusive and finicky they become. Large waters will always attract large crowds, which, given time, will always pressure the fish to the point of reluctancy and inactivity. Thus, if you are to be successful on such waters, you're going to have to find new and unique ways to catch them. This is why professional tournament anglers consistently catch fish, even though it's not always easy to do so.

And then there are the aesthetics of angling, the minute intricacies that have no direct effect on the fishing but certainly affect the overall experience of a day out on the water. For those of us who succumb to our primeval instincts, which urge us to explore the unexplored, to relish an hour of complete solitude, to see the forest in the trees, large waters seldom provide the fresh meat so necessary to sustaining our wild appetites. In order to satisfy such cravings, anglers of this school have to continually push the envelope of raw, soul-searing human need across a table of so-called "progress," a table supported by legs of urban development, pollution, technology, and a time of unprecedented popularity of fishing.

Occasionally, such a quest ends on a small, forgotten stream that has been omitted from all but the most detailed of maps, one that flows outside the boundaries of the rat race, one oblivious to the problems and pressures of our modern, fast-paced lives.

Small streams simply do not hold the numbers of fish found in large lakes, reservoirs, and rivers. Their size doesn't allow for it. Yet, like the large waters, these diminutive waterways often sustain lively ecosystems only on a smaller scale. A creek arm of a large reservoir may, at times, hold dozens or even hundreds of sexually mature female bass, but a given pool in a small stream may be home to only two or three at any one time. Despite this glaring variance, however, such a disparity is roughly proportionate.

For example, small streams don't harbor the number of

Small-stream bass don't grow as large as their lake-dwelling cousins, but they are every bit as capable of putting both you and your tackle to the ultimate test.

baitfish found in large waters. But they don't have to. The self-sustaining populations that do exist provide forage for the streams' predator fish, which are, as previously mentioned, fewer in number.

Another factor of small streams is the size of fish they support. Granted, there are almost always a few "trophies" within any given stream, but for the most part, the bass of such waters are smaller in size than their lake- and reservoir-dwelling counterparts—significantly so. Although much of this may be attributed to the genetics of different bass subspecies, there is also a direct correlation to the available forage (size, type, and abundance), climate (which determines the fish's effective growing season), and habitat within any given water.

As you may infer, a largemouth bass living in a 50,000-acre reservoir has a distinct growing advantage over a stream-run fish of the same species. The large-water fish, upon maturing to three or four years, might feed heavily on 4-inch gizzard shad. An abundance of such high-protein forage, as is typically found in most southern impoundments, for instance, greatly facilitates the growth of predator fish such as bass.

On the other hand, the stream bass may subsist on a variety of forage, including everything from small minnows to insects and crayfish. Although bass can and do make a living from these nutritious morsels, their growth rate often isn't on par with large-water fish. Of course, I'm not comparing Florida-strain largemouth with the northern variety, nor am I comparing fish in a south Georgia lake with those in a Maine creek, for such discrepancies would only exacerbate the difference in size.

But forage is only part of the puzzle. A lake-dwelling largemouth bass is able to move to substantially deeper water during summer and winter than the stream fish. This advantage, among other things, affords the lake fish greater protection

Tangling with wild bass on remote, unpopular streams
makes them all trophies.

from anglers and predators, ostensibly extending the fish's life
and size.

Yet, as typical as such instances may be, small waters and
large fish aren't mutually exclusive. Black bass are remarkably
adaptable creatures, able to subsist on a variety of aquatic life.
As most small streams are rich in insect, fish, and other life,
predators like bass are often afforded a diverse forage base.
When this element is combined with suitable habitat, the
likelihood of a stream harboring large bass becomes a distinct
possibility. Throw in another variable that is almost exclusive
to small streams, such as low to nonexistent fishing pressure,
and the chances of that stream producing trophy-size fish become excellent.

It is important to note, however, that a "trophy" fish found in a stream obviously differs from that of a lake or large river. An 8-pound largemouth might constitute trophy proportions for a Minnesota lake, whereas a small stream located in the same vicinity might hold a few 3- or 4-pound fish, which would certainly constitute exceptional growth for a tiny creek. The differences and similarities are quite apparent, but proportionate, to each habitat.

Now are you getting the idea?

Good. But hold up! First you have to *find* such a stream. After all, you won't often read about these places in your local newspaper's outdoor column.

One of the characteristics of many small streams is that they're located in remote locations. Owing to their diminutive size, these watercourses are frequently omitted from state maps and other publications. Often they flow through private land. But there are ways to work around such adversities. All you need is the desire.

Although many of these bass streams are indeed located far from modern civilization, there are also plenty of them flowing near major cities and suburbs. You may have even crossed over one of these places on your drive to work or home, perhaps hundreds of times, without ever considering its possibilities for fishing. Being conveniently located makes these streams a good place to start. After a preliminary investigation (evaluating a stream will be covered in detail in a later chapter), you can usually determine a good deal about a particular stream's qualities. If the place doesn't meet your criteria, mark it off your list and continue looking. In this case, at least you'll know.

The next step in locating suitable bass water is to buy a highly detailed map of your area. Such maps are readily available from many state, federal, and private sources. Among the best are the *Atlas and Gazetteer* maps offered by the DeLorme Mapping Company. Once you have a good map, study the key and learn to read it. When you've familiarized yourself with this valuable tool, begin scanning areas that you suspect hold such streams. Upon locating a likely waterway, consider its beginning and ending point. What is the length of the stream? Are there any tributaries? If so, how many, and what are they like? Where are their confluences with your stream? What are these areas like? Is this stream a tributary for a larger watercourse or a lake? What is the surrounding topography like? In what part of your state is this stream located? This should tell you a few things, including the type—and in some instances the size—of fish likely to be found there.

Another idea is to contact your state department of natural resources, fish and game, wildlife conservation, or whatever moniker by which they are locally known. Consult a fisheries biologist who works that area and query him or her regarding the stream in question. Likely they'll be able to provide you with some valuable information about your prospect. And don't worry that you may be tipping him or her off as to your newfound "honey hole." In all probability the stream has been fished long before you and probably always will be fished. Also, the biologist has likely investigated the stream at some point or another, as this is his or her job. The main thing to remember is that such streams are frequently unpopular with the crowds, and the more remote or inhospitable its location, the more unpopular the stream will be.

One other issue of finding suitable small streams for fishing is that of legal concern. Who owns the stream, and are you legally allowed to fish it? If the stream flows through some sort of public land, such as a state hunting preserve, you can almost bet that you'll have unrestricted access. On the other hand, if the adjoining land is privately owned—and much of it is—you have but one option: to find the landowner and ask permission. To that end, you can do a lot to further your case by offering to pick up trash, close gates, stay on established trails and roads, release the fish you catch, and generally doing everything you can to present yourself as a responsible angler. Ultimately, however, it is up to the landowner to grant permission. Should he or she refuse, your only alternative is to target another section of the stream and hit up another landowner. Above all, respect the property owner's decision. Trespassing charges or flying lead just aren't worth the chance of catching fish.

Worst case, you can always locate a new stream and start over. Remember that the more remote or small the stream, the more unpopular it is generally. And in the absence of crowds before you littering or abusing the property, the more likely is the landowner to grant you permission. Just be resourceful, persistent, and courteous to all landowners with whom you come in contact, and you'll get there.

Chapter 2

Tackle and Equipment for Fishing Small Streams

S MALL-STREAM ANGLERS are no longer forced to use second-class equipment as in years past. Today tackle manufacturers recognize both the importance and popularity of light gear and its applications. Consequently, this equipment has saturated the market and is very easy to find.

I'm often asked exactly which type of tackle—spinning, casting, or fly—is best for fishing small streams. Personally, I don't believe that there is a single best type of gear for all fishing situations. What performs best one day may not catch as many fish the next. I also believe that you can catch more fish by choosing the correct tackle for the specific situation rather than forcing a certain rod, reel, and lure to do every job. I enjoy fishing with each type of the aforementioned tackle and believe each has its advantages in certain situations. Therefore, it is my intention to discuss each of the three in detail in this chapter. Furthermore, the remainder of this book will be dedicated to explaining how you can catch more small-stream bass by using spinning, casting, and fly tackle.

SPINNING RODS

Of the three classes of tackle discussed here, spinning gear is perhaps the most commonly used among small-water bass anglers. And there is good reason for its popularity. Spinning outfits do a lot of things well: They're useful in tight quarters, they lend themselves to a variety of casting styles, and they're easy to use. But their greatest strength lies in their ability to cast small- to medium-sized lures, even into the wind, and drop them softly on the water.

Inasmuch as we're discussing the fishing of small streams, I would rate those spinning rods in the ultralight- to light-action category entirely commensurate with the scope of this book. Of course, depending on the particular stream, water level, size of lure, and other variables, there are times when a medium-light to medium-action rod is very useful.

Rod length is another matter. The ideal length of a spinning rod is different for everyone, but this characteristic should be governed by the size of the stream, surrounding obstacles, and personal preference. In certain situations, such as fishing tight, brushy streams, a 4½-foot spinning rod is ideal. When the stream opens a bit, allowing more space to cast and maneuver the rod, a 5-foot model is a good choice. And when fishing large, open pools, a 6-foot rod provides good leveraging and casting capabilities. On small streams, I never use a spinning rod longer than 6 feet, and unless I'm searching for only the largest fish, I usually opt for the diminutive 4½-foot ultralight model.

Probably the most important characteristic of a rod is its action. For spinning (and casting) rods, action denotes speed.

Even tiny bass, like this juvenile smallmouth, make for great sport on ultralightweight tackle.

The most obvious difference is that a slow rod will flex more than a fast rod. Slower-action rods are more forgiving of casting style and flaws, and offer an advantage when fishing with crankbaits because of their softer tips. If while using a crankbait you set the hook at the slightest sign of a strike, you're likely to pull the lure from the fish's mouth before the hooks become embedded. A slower-action rod helps to minimize this problem. The soft tip is more forgiving of such hasty motions, thereby keeping the lure in the fish's mouth for a longer time.

Faster rods, on the other hand, tend to be a bit more sensitive than those with slower actions. Sometimes, they are considerably more sensitive and transmit the slightest disturbance on the lure directly and instantly to your hand. The added stiffness of these rods offers more fish-fighting power. Fast-action rods are also more efficient for casting into the wind and for obtaining distance.

One of the main drawbacks of faster rods, however, is that they lack the pinpoint accuracy of slower rods. This apparent detriment is often mitigated once an angler has used his fishing rod enough to know its capabilities. Just remember that there is no substitute for practice or experience.

The action of a spinning rod determines the size of lure and line the rod can effectively handle. Although an ultra-light-action rod may be designed to cast lures weighing from $\frac{1}{32}$- to $\frac{1}{8}$ ounce, a medium-light-action model might perform best with $\frac{1}{8}$- to $\frac{3}{8}$-ounce lures. Ideally, you will first determine the size of lure you plan to use and then outfit yourself with a rod so designed to handle it. When fishing for black bass in small streams, I seldom use a lure heavier than $\frac{1}{4}$ ounce.

Spend some time inspecting several rods, testing the action of each, in order to find the one that best suits your individual taste and needs. You can make this as elaborate an undertaking as you wish, but there is absolutely no need to rush out and invest in a state-of-the-art spinning rod. These tools perform well on the water, but your reluctance to drop $200 or more should never cost you a single fish. What is important is that you obtain a sensitive rod that will allow you to keep tabs on your lure while it is underwater doing its work. Generally speaking, higher-modulus graphite rods are more sensitive than those of a lower-modulus construction. On the flip side, high-modulus rods are also more brittle and therefore less durable than their low-modulus counterparts.

When I look at a spinning rod—or, for that matter, any type of rod—the first thing I do is check the manufacturer's label on the rod's butt section. Here I look for two things: the manufacturer's name and the rod model. Because I've been at this game for a while, these two distinctions immediately tell me almost everything I need to know about the rod. Then, the only thing that I need to do is select the length and action that best suit my needs.

However, if you're new to fishing or selecting rods, then I would urge you to forget the rod's manufacturer and model number. The thing you need to do is handle the rod to determine whether it suits your needs. Most importantly, you should find the rod comfortable to hold and cast. After you've used a few dozen different rods out on the water, you'll begin to get a handle on the significance of a manufacturer and model number. But until you've used a particular rod, these things mean nothing.

Reel seats and guides are largely a matter of personal preference, because under the right hand, all can be made to work well. These features help define a rod's aesthetic attributes, but they also serve definite purposes. For example, Tennessee-style reel seats, composed of nothing more than two bands around the handle, are the simplest and lightest of all, but they aren't as secure and don't provide the positive lockdown that the standard uplocking seats do.

Similarly, single-foot guides are lighter than the double-foot variety, but they're not as strong. However, as we're dealing with small-stream bass, not grouper or blue marlin, the single-foot guides should serve you well. What's important is the quality of the wrapping job. When selecting a rod, it isn't a bad idea to examine the wraps. The thread should be tightly and neatly wound around the blank, and each guide foot should be protected with a solid and smooth coat of epoxy.

These are just some of the features that make each rod unique. Part of the fun is inspecting several models to determine what you like best. Just remember that you don't have to pay a premium to get a good rod for small-stream bass fishing. Simply inspect the rod and ask questions until you decide what's best for you.

CASTING RODS

Casting tackle, often called "bait-casting" tackle, is the most overlooked gear when it comes to fishing for bass in small streams. Most anglers associate this class of tackle with the large-water and trophy-bass fraternities. But as with spinning gear, manufacturers offer scaled-down versions of such big-bass equipment, which are appropriately suited to many small-stream applications. The greatest advantage of this sort of tackle is the gear's ability to cast medium to heavy lures with pinpoint accuracy. Casting tackle is also ideal for leveraging fish out of heavy cover.

As is the case with spinning tackle, casting rods for small streams are distinguished from their large-water counterparts primarily by their size. On small water, those sticks measuring from 5 to 6 feet in length are usually your best bet. There are several manufacturers today offering these miniature casting tools, most with actions very similar to their big brothers. And these small rods don't force you to sacrifice performance, either.

I find that a 5½-foot, medium-action model fills the bill for a small-stream casting rod quite nicely. Such rods generally have the ability to throw heavy (¼- to ⅝-ounce) lures, using line ranging in size from 6- to 14-pound test. They also possess the backbone to horse even large fish out of thick cover. It is important to note, however, that action varies from manufacturer to manufacturer. In other words, a medium-action rod from Manufacturer A might differ from the same model offered

Casting tackle is ideal for leveraging large fish from
heavy cover.

by Manufacturer B. Therefore, it is imperative that you examine a rod and its advertised line and lure-weight range before purchase to determine whether it adequately suits your
needs.

A faster-action (heavier) rod is often useful when targeting
large pools, where long casts may be required. Such rods also
help when wind is an issue, and they typically offer superb sensitivity. Rods with slower (softer) tips, on the other hand, are
usually better when fishing with crankbaits. The softer tip is
more forgiving when you feel the fish strike and quickly set the
hook. The result is more hook-ups. A faster rod, being stiffer
and less forgiving, often pulls the lure from the fish before the
hooks penetrate. This is why many professionals use slower
fiberglass or fiberglass-composite rods for their crankbait work.

Fishing with weedless jigs and soft-plastic baits, on the other hand, requires different attributes in a rod. Because such lures are usually fished slowly and directly on the bottom, an angler must constantly feel what the lure is doing in order to be successful. Naturally, a faster-action rod is often used for such work, as these rods tend to offer a bit more sensitivity than their slower (softer) counterparts. As faster rods possess less flex in the tip, they therefore offer greater hook-setting power, which is often necessary when using soft-plastic baits. And when you have 40 or 50 feet of monofilament line out in the water—when line stretch is likely to be a factor in any hook set—faster rods are preferable for getting the job done.

Ultimately, your choice of action will depend on your own individual preferences and fishing style. In most cases, however, a medium-action rod incorporates the best features of both slow and fast actions, and lends itself well to almost all small-stream situations requiring a casting rod.

Fly-Rods

If there is one class of tackle with followers who forsake all other methods, it is that of fly tackle. Fly-fishing appeals to the traditionalist, the minimalist, and the purist in all of us. Perhaps it is the feel of the line shooting through fingers and guides, slicing into the air in that perennially sought tight and parabolic arc that calls our name. Or maybe it's the lively feel of the rod bowing under the pressure of a fish. Whatever it is that so enamors us, fly-fishing is an entirely different sport, far removed from fishing with conventional tackle—and it's also exactly the same.

There are those devotees who will never part with their fly tackle, regardless of circumstances, but there are others who use it in conjunction with conventional tackle when the

Using a fly rod to work the deep side of the stream is effective at any time of year.

time, situation, and mood dictate. When fishing small waters for black bass, fly tackle shines when feather-soft presentations are necessary and when lies can only be probed by drifting your offering downstream toward the target. It is also instrumental when the fish are feeding on insects, which are never so adroitly imitated as when presented on the end of a long, thin leader, carried to target by a slick, tapered line.

Unlike conventional rods, the actions of which denote the classification of line and lure weight they are designed to handle, the action of fly-rods determines how far down the blank the rod flexes when loaded. Thus, a tip-flex or fast-action fly-rod bends only in the upper third (or upper quarter on some rods) of the blank when flexed. A midflex or moderate-action fly-rod bends about midway down the blank, and a full-flex or slow-action rod bends nearly to the grip when cast.

Individual fly-rods are further distinguished by the particular line weight they're designed to cast. This designation, along with the rod's individual action, is its DNA. For example, it is possible to get a midflex 10-weight saltwater fly-rod or a midflex 3-weight stick, which would be designed for short presentations with tiny flies. They both have the same taper—or action—relative to the individual rod, but they throw vastly different line weights, making each a unique tool. With spinning and casting tackle, this isn't the case. The actions of these rods constitute their genetic makeup and determine the rod's specific qualities.

The most important factor to consider when selecting a new fly-rod is your own casting style. As no two casting strokes are completely identical, it stands to reason, then, that a particular rod's inherent attributes will differ slightly—or significantly in some cases—from one person to the next. Here it is absolutely imperative that you test-cast the rod before laying out your hard-earned money. What looks great on paper may be an utter insult to your form and skill as a caster on the water. With fly-rods, you're far better off casting several different models and then comparing on paper those which pass your test.

Fishing small streams demands certain qualities in a fly-rod, just as it does with conventional rods. And as is the case with the latter, fly-rod manufacturers have filled this niche by offering dozens of different models, each varying in line weight, length, and action.

Short rods, measuring from 6 to 8 feet in length, are generally well suited to fishing small streams, especially those with tight casting lanes and plenty of shoreline trees and brush. The problem is that rods of such length are generally available only in lightweight, trout-sized line weights of 5 and less. Although such light-line weights are perfect for casting tiny nymphs and dry flies, they generally lack the power to throw larger bass flies.

Longer rods, which measure from 8 to 9 feet or more in length, are available in most line weights and also serve a purpose on small streams. Longer rods allow for longer casts and better line manipulation both during and after the cast. Although they can be cumbersome in tight, brushy conditions, they can suffice if the angler is willing to modify his or her casting technique.

As far as line weights go, those rods designed to handle line sizes 4 through 7 are generally ideal for small streams. A 4-weight fly-rod works in certain situations, when casting small streamers or nymphs. Five-weight rods are usually able to throw weighted nymphs and streamers and even light sinking lines, but a 6-weight is more versatile on the bass stream. Six-weight fly-rods have the power to cast decent-sized streamer patterns, poppers, and nymphs, and they possess the backbone to tame even large fish. A 7-weight rod is often helpful when throwing heavy crayfish patterns or large, wind-resistant poppers or streamers. Most good 7-weights can handle a 200- to 250-grain sinking line with ease, and these rods shine when you're pursuing big fish or dealing with unruly winds.

So how do you choose the right rod?

First, you determine the size of fly you wish to throw. If you think that you'll use mostly larger flies, such as size-2 streamer patterns, and heavy, sinking lines, then a 6- or 7-weight fly-rod is probably your best bet. As your flies decrease in size, lighter rods can be considered. There are times when I'll opt for a 4-weight fly-rod when fishing small streams, but in other instances, such as during spring when the water levels in the creeks are high and currents strong, I'll generally opt for

36   a 6- or 7-weight stick. If you can have only one fly-rod, then a 6-weight is almost always your best choice, as this is the most versatile line weight of all.

Once you've determined the size of fly you intend to use and the length of the rod that best suits your fishing situation, the next factor to consider is action. Tip-flex or fast-action rods excel when wind is a factor. They have the backbone to tame large fish and throw heavier or larger flies and lines. Such rods are a good choice when fishing deep water with heavy structure.

A midflex or moderate-action rod is generally easier to cast than one with a fast action. Moderate actions are more forgiving of casting errors, and they are incredibly smooth and accurate. These versatile rods are logical choices for many small-stream conditions, provided that the rod suits your casting style. For fly-fishing small streams for black bass, a mid-flex rod is probably your single best choice, as it lends itself well to a variety of situations.

Although full-flex or slower actions are great for delivering delicate presentations, I don't recommend them for black bass, unless, of course, you intend to target only very small fish.

Once you make the commitment and purchase a fly-rod, the single best thing you can do is to spend some time learning to cast. Invest the money in a casting lesson, for your time will be well rewarded. Once you master the basic overhand cast, practice different casting techniques, such as the roll cast, side-arm cast, and even the back cast. If you spend enough time on a stream, chances are that you'll need to draw on your skills with one of these casts, or others, in order to effectively deliver the fly to target.

REELS

Reels serve several purposes for the small-stream angler and indeed for fishers on any body of water. The most important functions are the reel's ability to store line, dispense the line when a fish makes a run, and retrieve the line. When fishing small streams, the latter task is more often associated with spinning and casting tackle, as fly-anglers often strip in line by hand. However, there are instances, especially when playing larger fish, when a fly-fisher might "put the fish on the reel" and therefore call on the reel to retrieve the line. Regardless of which type of tackle you prefer, it is imperative to buy a good reel, although it doesn't have to be expensive.

But what constitutes a good reel?

The single most important feature of a reel is its drag system. This feature, more so than any other, will determine the quality and value of the reel for the angler. Does the line come off the reel smoothly and without hesitation, skipping, or jerking? Is the drag knob conveniently located so as to provide easy access? How about the drag range? A good reel should have a wide range of drag settings, providing for everything from heavy drag to absolutely none.

These days, there is a great dispute among fly-fishers about the value and apparent superiority of pure cork as a drag material over other synthetic products. This may or may not be true, and although this may be an important consideration when fishing for king mackerel or wahoo, small-stream bass fishing doesn't necessitate or warrant the buying of a cork-drag reel—unless, of course, that is your wish. As these reels are generally quite expensive (I can think of only one manufacturer offering reasonably priced cork-drag reels), it should come as some comfort to you that this is an area in which you can save some money. Just ensure that your reel, regardless of

38 the material used, has a smooth, steady drag.

Similarly, don't concern yourself too much about whether a particular reel is machined or cast, extensively ported or not. These features do impart a certain aesthetic appeal to a particular reel, and they do serve a purpose for certain fishing situations, such as bluewater combat, but they simply aren't required for catching bass from small streams.

Inasmuch as the rod constitutes the majority of your tackle investment, the reel is one item on which you can save some money. Of course, if you have the resources and are so inclined, you might not be happy with anything but the best equipment. And this is certainly your prerogative. However, value will be a prime consideration for most anglers, and to that end, it is important that you get a good reel for your money.

Although you can spend upward of $200 on a spinning or casting reel, and more than double that on a top-of-the-line fly reel, please be advised that you can get a quality reel, of any type, for less than $150. And the price of a good spinning reel is often much less than that. You can go a long way in preserving your reel and getting the maximum service out of it if you take the time to wipe it down after each use. Also, periodically clean and oil your reel as needed. Remember that any time you completely submerge your reel in the water, it should be completely disassembled—the parts sprayed with a water-displacing solvent such as WD-40, dried, and then reoiled and polished up before storing. And regardless of the type of reel you use, always store it in a protective cover—even if it's nothing more than an old sock—when it's not in use.

Of course, you don't have to do any of this. I'm simply giving you a few suggestions for making your equipment last. These are measures that I take with my own equipment, and I have reels that I've used for more than twenty years that are still going strong today.

LINE

Fishing lines have, in recent years, progressed on pace with fishing rods, reels, and any other of today's high-tech tackle. With terms such as *polymer, copolymer, braided, hybrid,* and *fluorocarbon,* things can get confusing if you aren't familiar with today's fishing lines. But for fishing small streams with conventional tackle, all you really need to remember is *monofilament.*

Although it is true that many of the new or advanced lines have upped the ante in the abrasion-resistance and tensile-strength categories, it is equally true that these improvements shouldn't always preclude the use of traditional monofilament for many situations. For instance, I often use Berkley FireLine when fishing for walleye in deep lakes because of its incredible sensitivity and abrasion resistance. But in small streams, monofilament line works just fine. Here the fish are much shallower, and it's easier to detect strikes. Also, because the water is shallower, small-stream bass are often much more nervous and wary than lake fish. This often requires me to use a fine-diameter monofilament, as many low-stretch and braided lines would surely scare the fish.

By no means am I suggesting that you forsake your favorite line for monofilament 100 percent of the time; after all, if you have a favorite line, there is probably a reason for it. Maybe you have confidence in the line you use. So by all means, use that which gives you confidence. But remember that most fish aren't lost because a line lacked a certain tensile strength or abrasion resistance; most fish are lost because of poor knots, dull hooks, and old line, which are angler errors.

There is one new development in fishing line that I believe will help you to catch more fish in certain situations: the advent of fluorocarbon line. This line, in clear water, becomes practically invisible, as it absorbs sunlight rather than reflecting it. This decreased visibility often increases a fish's propensity to strike a lure. Fluorocarbon line also offers good abrasion resistance, but the main drawback is that such line is more expensive than traditional monofilament. I like to use fluorocarbon line in those situations in which the water is extraordinarily clear, but for probably 80 percent of my small-stream fishing, I opt instead for a low-visibility green monofilament, which closely matches the water color in the streams I typically fish.

As for line size, I use everything from 2-pound test all the way up to 10- or 12-pound test in certain situations. Obviously, the light line is beneficial when using ultralight spinning tackle with tiny jigs and grubs. It is also good in open pools or flats, which lack heavy structure.

The more structure—such as logs, brush, or boulders—a stream contains, the heavier the line I use. For example, if I'm throwing small spinnerbaits into a shallow, open pool, I'll typically go with a 6- or 8-pound-test line. But when tossing heavy jigs or soft plastics and working them through heavy cover along the bottom of a pool, I use 10- or 12-pound test.

The important thing to remember, regardless of the type of line you use, is to match the size of line to the size and weight of lure you're using. Obviously, heavy lines impede the actions of small lures, and light lines are at a risk of breaking when tied to heavy lures. Consider both the size and weight of lure you intend to use. This should give you an idea as to the correct size of line. Once you get a *rough estimate* on the ideal line size, allow the particular stream characteristics and conditions to lead you to the *correct* line size.

Fly lines are a different ball game altogether. Here you have the choice of a floating, intermediate (or slow-sinking), fast-sinking, and even a super-fast-sinking line. The latter three are available in the form of a full-sinking line, whereby the entire line sinks beneath the surface, or in sinking-tip models, in which only a portion of the line sinks while the running line floats or remains near the surface.

Fly lines are further distinguished from one another in their individual tapers. For example, a weight-forward fly line has a continuous forward taper, whereas a double taper has a larger belly, with tapers on either end. Another type of fly line is the shooting head. This incorporates a thin running line with a heavier head, which allows for maximum casting distance. However, shooting-head lines are largely impractical for fishing small streams.

For bass fishing in small streams, I like a weight-forward line for most situations. Weight-forward lines allow you to throw larger flies, and they handle the wind more efficiently than double-tapered lines. However, double-tapered lines excel in roll casting and line mending, which are two tricks of use on the bass stream.

The most versatile line for fishing small streams is certainly the floating line. Such lines allow you to effectively target the first 4 or 5 feet in the water column and are great when the fish are shallow. With these lines you can even work deeper simply by lengthening and weighting your leader.

Another good option for small waters is a sinking-tip line. With most of these lines, the tip section sinks beneath the surface while the running line floats and remains visible to the angler (some sinking-tip lines are now available with an intermediate-sinking running line), thereby allowing you to monitor your fly. Sinking tips are good for fishing deep pools, ledges, and runs, where the fish may be holding at 5 or 6 feet below the surface.

Full-sinking lines are also useful on small waters and are

best used in the deepest pools when working a fly slowly across the bottom is desired. These lines are frequently beneficial during the winter, when the fish are lethargic and holding in deep water. When using a sinking line, remember to shorten your leader so as to allow your fly to descend in the water column.

One of the great things about using different fly lines is that you don't have to invest in several different fly reels in order to be prepared for any given situation. Simply carry an extra spool or two, each equipped with a different line, and interchange them as you see fit.

WADERS

There are a variety of wader styles and materials these days, each well suited to use in streams. And with the recent advent of the breathable models, it is possible to fish year-round in complete comfort. Breathable waders generally incorporate a waterproof (and breathable) layer, which is then covered and protected by subsequent outer layers. Some models simply feature a water-resistant coating, which reduces cost, but which also deteriorates over time. Because breathable waders are generally lightweight in construction, they are ideal for warm-weather fishing. Yet, when the weather turns cold, you can simply add layers of insulation in the form of fleece or wool pants to provide added comfort.

Neoprene waders—although they don't breathe—offer superior cold-weather protection. Such waders are available in several different weights, often ranging from 2mm to 5mm in thickness. Obviously, the latter would be best for the coldest conditions. Such waders are heavier than the breathable models, but they are also extremely comfortable and flexible, which you'll notice anytime you kneel down to release a fish.

Neoprene waders are moderately priced, and with the proper care, they provide years of service.

One note about neoprene waders: Inasmuch as these waders do not breathe, condensed body vapors are likely to accumulate, resulting in moisture on the inside. Once your clothes become laden with this moisture, you are likely to get cold. Therefore, it is wise to wear moisture-wicking pants or underwear beneath your neoprene waders. This is important to the comfort of those wearing breathable waders, but it is absolutely necessary to those fishing in neoprenes for a prolonged period of time. Moisture-wicking garments ensure that the body remains warm and dry.

Vinyl or rubber waders are the least expensive of all and simply provide a waterproof barrier between you and the stream. These waders are sometimes constructed of a single layer of material, whereas other models often incorporate protective outer layers. These waders do not breathe, nor do they stretch as do neoprenes. Consequently, they are usually best suited for use during spring or fall, when the water is just a bit too cool for wet-wading.

Waders are available in boot-foot or stocking-foot models. Boot-foot waders incorporate a waterproof boot and are easy and quick to don or shed. Stocking-foot waders, on the other hand, require the use of an additional, protective boot over the wader. They take a bit more time to slip on, but these waders and their boots usually provide additional comfort not found in the boot-foot variety.

Speaking of boots, it is always advisable to wear wading boots when wading a stream. These boots are designed to protect your feet from sharp rocks, stickups, and other underwater hazards. Naturally, they should feature a durable and solid sole, as well as a hard, protective toe box.

The sole of your boots is yet another consideration. Here

44   you have your choice of lug, felt, spiked, or even rubber "gripper" soles. The last often incorporate small suction cups for added traction on slippery rocks. These soles are usually more durable than felt soles and are a logical choice when you have to hike a considerable distance in your waders before reaching your fishing destination.

Felt soles are similar to having carpet glued to the bottom of your boots. This material affords you good traction on wet, slippery rocks. However, felt soles wear rapidly and must be continually replaced.

When you frequently encounter slippery, moss-covered rocks, felt soles that incorporate metal studs or spikes are a good choice. Such soles provide maximum traction when the footing is precarious. They cost more than standard felt soles, but when the situation warrants, they are well worth the money.

Finally, lug soles are available as an option, especially on boot-foot waders. Lug soles are usually made of a hard rubber and provide good traction in muddy or sandy conditions. Be advised, however, that they are not intended for use on slippery rocks!

Another option in the wader department is the hip boot. Hip boots, as the name implies, generally reach to a person's thighs or just below the hips. These waders are ideal for working shallow water, and they allow you to stay relatively cool during warm weather.

As a final option, you can always wet-wade a stream should you find the water temperature to your liking. This can be a comfortable and pleasant way to work a stream in the heat of summer, and an inexpensive one. In any event, always remember to wear a good pair of boots, even when wet-wading.

WATERCRAFT

It is my opinion that boats, canoes, and other watercraft are impractical for most small-stream fishing situations and are best left to the rivers and other large waters. Still, there are some instances when wading or fishing from the bank are next to impossible, and the only way to access an area is by boat.

Aluminum boats are sometimes used by small-water anglers, particularly when fishing long, deep pools. These boats allow one to penetrate areas that are completely inaccessible to wading or shore-bound anglers. They're also relatively inexpensive and are great for storing extra gear, such as camping equipment, when an overnight stay is planned. On the downside, however, they are often heavy and cumbersome to maneuver over many small waters. And when filled with gear, they can be difficult to portage.

A logical alternative to the metal boat is the canoe, which is highly popular with many river and stream anglers. Canoes are generally lightweight and simple to operate, usually requiring no electric motors or outboard engines. Consequently, they're much easier to portage over rocks or logs.

The drawback to canoes is their lack of stability in the water. Although they're a good choice to reach tight or deep areas of a stream, canoes can be prone to capsizing and spilling your gear into the water, especially in areas of heavy or rough current. However, a familiarity with your craft, its limitations, and experience on the water will help prevent such hazards.

An alternative to boats and canoes is a float tube. This sort of watercraft, which is nothing more than a vinyl- or nylon-covered inner tube with pockets, is the simplest and least expensive of all. Furthermore, it is easy to carry over shallow riffles and along narrow streamside trails. The down-

46   side is that if the tube punctures, you're out of the floating business, at least temporarily.

If I were forced to choose one of the aforementioned for accessing deep pools, it would be the float tube. However, many such pools are accessible with the right rod if you spend a little time searching and contemplating before going into action.

As you may infer, I feel that the best way to explore a small stream is on foot. This method is the simplest, requiring the least equipment, and if done properly, it can be the most stealthy mode of all. Some situations will require you to fish from the bank, which is often advisable, but most of your small-stream endeavors can be accomplished by slow, methodical wading.

Chapter 3

Stocking a Tackle Box for the Small Stream

O NE OF THE JOYS of gearing up for a fishing adventure is selecting the appropriate tackle for your intended destination and quarry. Today, there is such a stunning array of fishing lures and flies on the market that you can spend hours deciding which offerings to use. For some, this may be a painstaking ordeal, whereas others relish the thought of poring over this vast selection in anticipation of selecting just the right lures and flies to catch fish.

The old boy scout motto "Be Prepared" has a good deal of significance and relevance for anglers, whether fishing small waters, large rivers, or lakes. Of course, the basic premise here is to have a sufficient variety of baits on hand with which to trigger strikes on any given day. Some days may require the use of small, minnow-imitating plugs or flies, whereas soft plastics, spinners, or nymph patterns may be the ticket on the next day.

So how do you go about selecting just the right tackle for the job?

First you consider your quarry and then your destination. Of course, we're after black bass. And because we're talking about small streams, we realize, then, that the fish we're seeking are generally smaller than those found in large lakes or reservoirs. *Most* of them, that is.

Let's begin by outfitting ourselves for fishing small streams with conventional tackle.

I start by first selecting the tackle box that I intend to use. Am I referring to a large, bulky five-drawer megabox? Certainly not. We're fishing small streams here and generally wading them, not working large lakes with a boat. This means that your tackle box should be small and easy to carry. I like the small, multicompartment plastic boxes, such as those offered by Plano. In fact, I use one for soft plastics, one for jigs, one for spinners, and another for plugs. I'll also carry a separate, smaller box for hooks and sinkers. In certain situations, I carry my flies in these small, easy-to-see-into boxes as well.

Where do I carry all these boxes? I generally stuff them into the pockets on my fishing vest or in my waders. And I don't often take along this many boxes; many times I'll combine several different lures into a single box. Whatever you decide to do, just be organized about it, so that you can maximize your fishing time.

Next comes the actual lure selection. But first, we have to understand what we're trying to imitate with our bait. This is when scouting a stream pays off. Is your stream full of minnows, sunfish, or other baitfish? How about invertebrates like crayfish? Notice any frogs, snakes, or small mammals, such as mice, scurrying about the banks? Well, good. Then you certainly have an idea as to what the bass in your stream eat.

Let's talk about soft plastics.

Soft-Plastic Baits

I love soft plastics because they are so versatile and effective. You can rig them so many different ways, many of them weedless, which is necessary for working thick cover. They're also inexpensive. But most of all, soft-plastic baits *work*!

I would begin by selecting an assortment of plastic worms. You can use any color you like, but always include black in your selection. Other good colors include chartreuse, pumpkinseed, watermelon, grape, motor oil, red, and white. Of course, there are many others. Choose a few smaller worms, maybe something in the 3- to 4-inch range, and some larger ones, to 7 inches or so. You can also diversify your stock by picking worms with different tail shapes or perhaps some of those with ribbed bodies. Just make sure you have several different sizes, colors, and styles in your box.

Next stop is the grub department. You should have already placed a package of 2-inch curly-tailed grubs in your shopping cart, but feel free to buy the 1- or 3-inch variety if you see fit. The three most important colors are black, white, and chartreuse.

You'll also need some jig heads for these grubs, so buy some in black or white. Buy several sizes, from $\frac{1}{16}$ ounce up to $\frac{1}{8}$ or even $\frac{1}{4}$ ounce, because you'll use all of them. When you get home, remember to clean the paint out of the eye, and check the points on those hooks. Sharpen them until they dig in when slid across your thumbnail.

Next comes tubes. Tubes are remarkable baits, renowned for their ability to trigger strikes when nothing else seems to work. Your tackle box should include an assortment of the small, 2- to 3-inch tubes, as well as a few of the larger 4-inch models. Again, black and white are essential colors, but in many waters, pumpkinseed, root beer, and watermelon are also excellent choices. Once you have these basic colors in place, expand on them any way you like.

Finally, you'll want to add a few crayfish patterns to your box. Buy these in several sizes and colors, and use them. They work.

For use with your soft plastics, you'll want to stock up on hooks and sinkers. The size of hooks you use will depend on the size of baits you throw and the size of fish you expect to catch. For worms, I generally use a 1/0 off-shanked worm hook, but for tubes, especially the larger ones, you may want to try a 2/0 or 3/0 wide-gap hook. The wider gap will often help you avoid gut-hooking a fish.

Your sinker selection should include some BB-sized and smaller split shot, as well as some ⅛- to ¼-ounce bullet and barrel sinkers, the latter for Carolina rigs.

Glass beads and other noisemakers are sometimes helpful, particularly in muddy water. In small streams, I've found that the fish generally find my soft-plastic bait when I make a well-placed cast. But use the noisemakers if you must.

This completes the foundation for your soft-plastics box. Feel free to experiment with different styles, colors, and sizes to determine what works best for your particular stream.

The next box we'll fill is that for your spinnerbaits.

Spinnerbaits

Very simply, spinnerbaits produce well because they appeal to the fish's sense of sight, sound, and vibration. They may be retrieved quickly or slowly, jigged vertically, or pulled horizontally. Additionally, they work in most any depth of the water column, from the surface to the bottom. Spinnerbaits work

Diversify your fly selection for the small stream, but always bring plenty of streamer patterns.

well at any time of year, but in the springtime and early summer, they work wonders.

My favorite spinnerbait for small-stream bass is a ⅛-ounce model in white, chartreuse, or a combination of these colors. Sometimes, I'll use a lure that incorporates orange, red, or black, but for most daytime conditions, the white and chartreuse models produce best for me. Have several of these on hand with both Colorado and willow-leaf blades.

Occasionally, I'll throw a slightly larger, ¼-ounce spinnerbait if I suspect the possibility of catching an exceptionally large fish, but most of the time I leave the heavier baits at home with my large-water gear.

In-line spinners are incredibly useful in small streams and consistently produce well for all species of black bass. I prefer those with a dressed tail in order to give the fish something additional to target. When using an ultralight rig, you'll probably find the $\frac{1}{16}$-ounce size most useful, but $\frac{1}{8}$-ounce models are great for slightly heavier equipment. Have several on hand, in different colors, with both silver and gold blades.

Additionally, it isn't a bad idea to incorporate some of the baitfish-imitating plugs, which feature spinners, into your selection. Blue Fox® offers a variety of such lures, many of which have produced well for me. Outfit your box with a few $\frac{1}{8}$- and $\frac{1}{4}$-ounce models. This completes your spinnerbait box. Plugs are next.

PLUGS

Plugs—correctly identified as crankbaits, stickbaits, or sometimes top-water baits—are some of the easiest and most exciting lures to use. These lures typically imitate minnows or other baitfish, although some are designed to mimic crayfish, frogs, and other creatures. As baitfish are one of the foundations of a healthy bass stream, crankbaits and stickbaits should compose something of a base for your tackle selection.

Crankbaits are one lure category in which you can easily get confused, because there are so many good ones available on the market. We can divide crankbaits into two categories: lipless and lipped. Lipless crankbaits, such as the Rat-L-Trap, are very streamlined in appearance and effectively mimic baitfish such as shad, shiners, or minnows. These lures are great for burning through the water or even for jigging. Often, they incorporate rattles inside the body to help attract fish. Of the lipless variety, you are wise to incorporate several of the $\frac{1}{8}$- and $\frac{1}{4}$-ounce sizes into your selection. Choose a va-

The author's father with a bass taken on a lipless crankbait.

riety of colors, including orange, chartreuse, silver, gold, and any other shade you can find. You can't go wrong with these baits, and you can never have too many. If you fish enough, there will be a time and sky and water condition for all of them.

Lipped crankbaits feature a lip, which displaces water, causing the lure to move erratically, like an injured baitfish. These lips are also designed to help a lure run at a certain depth in the water column. Lipped crankbaits come in shallow-running, middepth, and deep-running varieties, depending on the shape and size of the lip. For small streams, forget the deep-running lures, as seldom will you need to reach down below 5 or 6 feet in the water. Instead, stock up on several sizes and colors of shallow- and middepth-running

54   lures. Again, the ⅛-ounce size is primo, but ¼-ounce lures aren't too big.

The same colors mentioned for the lipless crankbaits also work well for the lipped variety. And always keep a few crayfish-colored patterns on hand.

Stickbaits are elongated lures that imitate minnows and other baitfish. These lures are generally best used either on or just beneath the surface, down to 3 or 4 feet. Of course, you can go much deeper than that, but there is really no point in doing so. Stickbaits, being the large-profile lures that they are, are sight baits. They trigger fish into striking as a result of their large silhouettes and flashy colors. Stickbaits bring fish up from deeper water, often a considerable distance. Consequently, we don't use these baits on the bottom, where their inherent qualities would go unnoticed by many fish. You'll also lose a lot of lures this way.

Some stickbaits are also known as *jerkbaits*. As the name implies, jerkbaits lend themselves well to a quick, jerking action on the retrieve, which imparts an erratic movement to the lure, thus simulating an injured or crippled bait fish. These lures come in both floating and suspending varieties, and both are designed to work high in the water column. Bass will come from far off to nail a well-manipulated jerkbait.

Some stickbaits are floaters, designed for top-water work. Again, these lures imitate dying or struggling baitfish, floundering about the surface. Quick jerking or popping retrieves usually best manipulate this sort of lure.

For small-stream fishing, you are wise to select a variety of such lures ranging in size from an inch to perhaps 4 or 5 inches. Chartreuse, fire-tiger, clown, and shad colors produce well all across the country, though there may be other shades better suited to your individual stream. It is wise to incorporate a few suspending models with your floaters, as both will eventually have their days in the sun.

That does it for the plug box. Next comes one of my favorite lures: weedless jigs.

WEEDLESS JIGS

Weedless jigs, of any size and color, are big-bass medicine. They are also some of the most consistent producers because they demand a slow, tantalizing presentation, which is often necessary to entice larger fish to strike. They imitate a variety of aquatic life, but it's usually crayfish that they most effectively mimic.

Go with two sizes of jigs—⅛- and ¼-ounce—and always have plenty of black, white, orange, and brown on hand.

Don't forget the pork trailers, either. I like pork because it imparts a realistic taste and texture to the fish. Once committed to striking, pork entices the fish to hold onto the lure longer, thus increasing your chances of a successful hook-up. Additionally, in cold water (below 50 degrees Fahrenheit), pork undulates very naturally, unlike plastic trailers. Black, white, brown, blue, and even orange are all good colors for pork trailers.

Now your jig box is full. Wasn't that simple?

FLIES

Next, I'd like to talk a little bit about putting together a fly box for small-stream bass. Essentially, it's the same game as with conventional lures, except that flies are generally concocted from fur, feathers, and other "crafty" materials, and the end product then is designed to appeal primarily to a fish's sight.

56   As is always the case, fly-anglers must put in the time scouting or studying a stream to get a grip on what foods are available to its bass. Please note that you'll also need an assortment of split-shot weights to get a fly down to a desired depth, along with a selection of different tippet sizes for throwing various sizes of flies.

Let's begin with top-water flies.

Surface Flies and Bugs

Surface bugs—or *poppers* as they're commonly called—are logical choices for the small-water bass angler. These flies can be made to imitate a struggling baitfish floating on the surface, or they may mimic a frog kicking across the water. Poppers, when properly manipulated, sputter, gurgle, or pop, thereby alerting any nearby predator fish. These flies may be fished in a variety of situations but are generally most effective when worked around weed beds and other vegetation early or late in the day.

Brightly colored poppers perform very well in most situations, but during low-light periods, black is your best bet. Naturally, your fly box should include several popper patterns in sizes ranging from about a 6 to a 2, or even 1/0. Larger poppers will generally require the backbone of a 6- or even a 7-weight fly-rod to put into motion, along with a fairly stout leader and a line so tapered to deliver such wind-resistant offerings.

And then there are top-water flies, or *dry flies*, as they're commonly known. Dry flies are generally regarded as synonymous with trout, but they can certainly work wonders on small-stream bass.

I mentioned earlier that small-water bass are opportunists, and as such, they take advantage of any and every available food source. Most small streams are extremely rich in insect life, both aquatic and terrestrial forms. And regardless of where you live, it is guaranteed that insects of some

Baitfish-imitating flies are always a good bet for the small stream.

form or another exist in your small stream. These may include mayflies, caddisflies, dragonflies, damselflies, crickets, grasshoppers, moths, or many others. Sounds like a trout's diet, I know, but bass are accustomed to seeing these insects and eating them.

Consequently, it's a good idea to bring along a good variety of dry flies to the bass stream. Don't be afraid to try them in larger sizes, either. For example, many areas of the country, especially the Midwest, are beset with large grasshoppers from summer to fall. Fish a size-6 hopper pattern near your stream's grassy banks along about August or September, and rest assured that if any fish are present, your fly will soon be demolished.

In-line spinners are terrific smallmouth medicine, year-round.
(Photo by Jay Armstrong)

Of course, old trout standbys such as the Royal Coachman, Adams, and Royal Wulff in sizes 10 or 12 can be terrific producers for bass. Equally as productive are damselfly and white miller imitations. Like trout, bass aren't afraid to come up and nail a skating or drifting dry fly.

And don't think that ant and beetle patterns are restricted to the trout streams, either.

Streamers

Streamers are subsurface flies that mimic everything from leeches to minnows and other baitfish. Probably the most popular streamer pattern is the woolly bugger, which will catch virtually anything that swims. Other good ones include minnow patterns, such as the Clouser Deep Minnow, and baitfish- or shad-imitating patterns, such as the Lefty's Deceiver.

Streamers may be fished with a quick or slow strip, or a series of strips; they may be fished shallow or deep; and they may even be drifted below a strike indicator. Naturally, these versatile flies are staples of the well-stocked small-stream fly box.

With woolly buggers and similar patterns, it is wise to carry an assortment ranging in size from 10 to 4 or so. Black, brown, white, purple, chartreuse, and olive are all wonderful colors, especially those that are tied with crystal chenille, a bead head, and a few strands of Krystal Flash in the tail.

Bait-fish imitations should always be on hand in sizes ranging from about 8 through 1. If you tie your own, it is helpful to tie some with weed guards to help avoid snags when working near heavy cover. Some of the best colors for bait-fish imitations are solid white, chartreuse/white, gray/white, brown/orange, red/gray, and solid black. Of course, feel free to experiment with different colors as you wish.

Nymphs are another useful type of fly when fishing for black bass in small streams. Like trout, stream-run bass feed heavily on these aquatic insects and will usually take a convincing imitation when presented properly. Most nymphs are best fished dead-drift or swing-drift style, beneath a strike indicator. As is the case when trout fishing, avoiding drag in your drift is one of the most important factors to getting strikes. Getting your fly deep enough is another. To accomplish the former, your fly line is simply mended upstream in order to avoid any pull on the leader and fly. Depth is attained with the addition of split shot or some other weight onto the leader.

In most streams, bass are accustomed to feeding on many varieties of nymphs, so it makes sense for you to carry an as-

Flies designed to be worked on or near the stream bottom, such as crayfish and sculpin imitations, are equally effective for large trout and bass.

sortment in your fly box. Some of the best patterns include stonefly nymphs, hellgrammites, and dragonfly and damselfly nymphs. For black bass, the best sizes usually range from 10 or 12 to 6 or so. Once again, what is important in nymph fishing is that you fish the fly very close to the stream bottom, where the fish are accustomed to seeing the naturals. At certain times, nymphing can be surprisingly effective for black bass.

Specialty Flies

Other flies, which may be classified here as specialty flies, are frequently of use on the small stream. These include crayfish patterns, of which you should always carry a good selection in sizes ranging from 8 to 2; divers, which imitate frogs, or in some cases, baitfish, and which may be used with a floating or sinking line, in sizes 8 through 2; sculpin patterns in sizes 8 to as large as 2 or so; and even a mouse or rat pattern in sizes 8 to 4.

There you have a fairly well-rounded fly box, which should offer you enough of a selection that you can catch bass under almost any circumstances. Now you must learn where and how to use these flies and conventional lures, which we'll discuss in a later chapter.

Chapter 4

Denizens of the Creeks and Streams

S MALL STREAMS frequently harbor a stunning array of fishes, from tiny minnows and sculpins to shad, shiners, darters, chubs, mad toms, and many other baitfish. Often, the same stream is home to an equally diverse predator-fish population, including such species as the largemouth, smallmouth, and spotted bass. As the scope of this book focuses on these three species, all of which are black bass (and which are not true bass but members of the sunfish family), let's examine how these fish adapt and behave within a small-stream environment.

Creeks, brooks, and other small streams have a good deal in common with larger waters, such as lakes, reservoirs, and rivers. For instance, in both waters there is a certain number of baitfish (or forage) and a certain number of predator fish, all coexisting within a given area. Granted, the given area of a small stream is substantially smaller than that of a lake, reservoir, or river, but a certain habitat boundary exists,

Black bass are found in small streams nationwide. Find one that offers a healthy forage base, cover, and a constant supply of water and you're in business.

nonetheless. And whether the forage fish would admit it or not, something of a symbiotic relationship exists between baitfish and predators.

The baitfish provide high-protein forage for predator fish, which, in turn, keep the numbers of baitfish in check by feeding on them. By doing so, the predators help prevent the baitfish from exceeding a particular water's carrying capacity.

But like the baitfish, bass also suffer from predation from time to time. On a large and popular lake, their enemies may include larger fish; raptors, such as eagles and ospreys; anglers; or the occasional virus, such as the largemouth bass virus.

In a stream, where the fishing pressure is often greatly re-

duced and the threat from anglers is less of a factor, bass still
have to contend with the threat of predation from hawks, raccoons, mink, weasels, otters, foxes, bears, and even extremes
in the weather. After all, stream fish can't move down into 50
feet of water to spend the winter; consequently, they must seek
out areas of relative comfort, such as those near springs or in
deep pools. So as you can see, there is plenty for a small-
stream bass to avoid, even though its home stream might not
see two dozen anglers in a year's time.

Small-water bass quickly learn that in order to avoid
danger, they must continually inhabit the safety of deeper
water. This is why deep, shady, brushy, tree-choked, and struc-
ture-infested pools almost always hold good numbers of fish,
both large and small. The fish instinctively relate to the safety
of deep water because they know that here they are safe from
the clutches of a raccoon or a raptor's talons. Yet, at certain
times of the year—such as spring—the fish are instinctively
guided to the shallows for spawning.

Like wise, old, and wary buck deer during the rutting
season, wise old bass forsake safety in order to fulfill their biological obligation of species propagation. Like the rutting
season for deer, spawning takes place over a relatively short
span of time, after which the fish leave the beds and return to
the safety of deeper water. Aside from the spawn, bass—especially larger bass—typically inhabit shallow water only for
very brief periods and then primarily during times of low light,
such as mornings, evenings, and nights. The remainder of the
time, which constitutes most of their lives, is spent in the
safety of deeper water, on or near structure and cover.

Given this, let's examine what these fish do when they're
holding in deep water, which is, after all, most of their lives.

Unlike open-water fish such as striped bass, black bass
don't chase down schools of baitfish or herd them up 40 or 50

Small-stream bass have many potential predators, including raptors, such as this bald eagle.

feet to the surface to feed on them. Of course, black bass are capable of doing almost anything for food, but for the most part, this doesn't constitute typical behavior.

Rather, black bass ambush their prey, often with swift, sudden, and efficient movements, so as to maximize net gain without spending undue energy. It follows then that these fish should be found inhabiting the same general area as their forage base, which is true. Obviously, if your garden is located right outside your back door, you won't have to expend much energy gathering food. Going to the grocery store on the other side of town will require much more effort. This is why locating baitfish—whether in a lake, pond, or stream—generally indicates that the predator fish are not far off. They must stay with their gardens because they ensure consistent and convenient supplies of food. And when times are hard, that trip to the supermarket on the other side of town to look for food might cost the predator fish its life.

Sometimes, this "garden" is located in the very same pool as that inhabited by the bass. Perhaps there are minnows hanging around weed edges, frogs leaping and swimming from a stand of lily pads over to the bank, sculpins scurrying on the stream bottom, and darters holding in the shallow water near the pool's tail. In this case, the garden would be located directly inside the bass's house. This, of course, would be the most convenient situation of all, which is why pools bearing such characteristics are prime holding areas for bass.

But maybe things aren't this convenient for the bass in your stream. Maybe a certain pool holds only a few forage fish, some small insects and invertebrates, and little else. But just below the pool is a flat, bordered on the opposite side by riffles. Perhaps this flat is home to several different species of forage fish, crayfish, frogs, and insects. In this case, the fish's garden is located in its backyard. Although not as convenient as having food right in your living room, this situation isn't too far from ideal. In this instance, however, a certain amount of risk is involved when the bass move onto the shallow flat to feed.

A bass leaves the safety of deep water and, upon entering the shallows, becomes an easy target for its many enemies. But black bass, especially larger ones, have learned to deal with this apparent adversity by listening to their instincts, which tell them to move into shallow water only during times of extremely low light (unless spawning). Not only do they feel safer and less exposed under low-light conditions, but during such times, the bass's eyesight is superior to that of its prey. And prey is exactly what these fish are looking for when they're found in shallow water early or late in the day. This is why fishing is usually best during these times; it is simply a case of being on the water during a productive time.

As a bass moves into shallow water, its instincts also urge it to take advantage of any available cover or structure. This might be a set of lily pads or a weed line near the edge of a flat, where a bass could position itself for an ambush party on its prey while simultaneously enjoying protection from predators.

And yet another favorite trick of prowling bass is to re- main in the deepest available water for as long as possible. That is, they avoid exposing themselves until they absolutely have to. Thus, anytime you encounter a situation in which deep water abuts an area of shallow water, it is worth your time to investigate.

Some years ago I witnessed the importance of such a situ- ation as I watched a very large and mature smallmouth bass stalk a school of baitfish. I was fishing a small stream in the Ozarks of southern Missouri, working a relatively shallow area between two deep pools. It was early morning, and the stream was shaded by the many oak and sycamore trees on the bank. About 10 yards ahead I could see a school of large minnows hugging the edge of a weed bed near the shoreline. Upon seeing these baitfish, I went to work replacing my fly with a minnow pattern in hopes of connecting with any nearby bass.

Moments later, movement across the stream caught my eye. I noticed a dark, elongated shape cruising upstream, somehow unaware of my presence. There it paused, and I was so taken with the appearance of a large fish in such shallow water that I just watched it for a moment. I was too close to cast, as any movement on my part would have surely alerted the fish.

I could see the big fish fanning its fins, adjusting its posi- tion ever so subtly, and I knew it had locked on to the school of baitfish, which was still in place near the stream bank. I could see the dark vertical bars and the lighter, blotchy green and brown patches identifying the fish as a smallmouth, for it was quite close at this point.

Suddenly, the fish shot forward like a deployed torpedo, bearing down on the minnows and causing a huge, V-shaped wake on the surface. In the time it takes to blink an eye, the smallmouth had assaulted the school of baitfish, sending minnows leaping from the water in every direction, grabbed a meal, and then turned and shot back to the far side of the stream. Actually, it took about three seconds. I then watched as the dark mass glided back downstream from whence it came, soon disappearing into the pool.

Wondering why the fish had moved up the far side of the stream, I waded over and found a small ditch, which ran parallel to the bank and which was perhaps a foot deeper than the shallow side where I had been standing. I found that the miniature channel ended at precisely the point where the smallmouth had paused and poised itself for the attack. And thus was my firsthand introduction to the hunting habits of cagey and shrewd bass, the ones that have to leave the comfort of home to go and get food from a nearby garden.

Although at times even the largest of fish will leave the safety of deep water in search of food, most learn that they are better off remaining in deep, fertile pools. By using the term *learn*, I don't mean to imply that fish are intelligent in the way humans are. Most fish have incredibly small brains and don't rely on a thought process as do you and I. Rather, they are driven by powerful instincts that dictate their behavior. These instincts have been refined over thousands of years. Those that didn't evolve these instincts didn't live very long, thus ensuring that only the strong and wary survive.

At any rate, a bass has relatively few basic needs. The most important of these are food and shelter. Food comes in the form of insects, invertebrates, amphibians, other fishes, and even small mammals, such as mice. Shelter, then, takes the form of water—*deep* water—and cover. The adjective *deep* is a relative term, and when used to describe water within a small stream, it may actually contradict the same word used to describe a lake, reservoir, or river. Thus, *deep* often means *deepest*.

Many small streams average perhaps less than 3 feet in depth, though frequently there are pools, holes, and runs with much deeper water, sometimes 6 feet or more. Of course, this is different for every stream, and there are always exceptions. But let's say your small stream has a couple of pools that are 5 feet at their deepest point, whereas the rest of the stream runs from 1 to 3 feet deep. Presumably, a forage source of some type is found throughout the stream, whether this is microscopic plankton, tiny insects, small fish, larger fish, or invertebrates. And provided that there is a food source available within a certain area of the stream for *one* size and type of fish, chances are that the presence of such a fish will attract others. For example, if a shallow flat below a pool is home to large numbers of insects, then chances are that small baitfish, which feed on these insects, will be found here. Consequently, the baitfish will attract predators at some point or another.

Almost any area within a stream can and will hold bass at some point or another. These may not be the largest bass, and they may be relatively few in number, but chances are that some of these fish may be found, at some point in time, on any section of stream. This is why stream anglers often catch many fish, many of them small in size, over the course of the stream. There are almost always bound to be fish scattered throughout a certain habitat.

Then there are the larger fish, those that remain primarily in the sanctuary of the deeper pools. Likely, these pools hold an abundance of aquatic life, which serves the bass's need for food. This may be due to the given structure within a pool; the various characteristics of the pool, such as its water depth, available vegetation, or bottom composition; or its position below a falls or riffles, which would ensure the pool a constant supply of food, thanks to the current.

But equally important is shelter. For what good to a bass is food without shelter? Shelter is often described as *structure*, which may include an infinite number of things, but which is really nothing more than an interruption or variance of habitat. This may include an old log lying at the bottom of a pool, a rock ledge, a gravel bar, a weed bed, an unusually large boulder lying beside a run, a deadfall, an eddy, an undercut bank, a brush pile, a bottom depression carved out by the force of the water, overhanging limbs, a waterfall, or many, many other things within a certain body of water. Structure, then, is simply something different that attracts fish. Fish always gravitate to that different something, which is why you should do the same when fishing.

But not all structure provides shelter for fish. To fill this need, we need to look for what is often called *cover*. Under the right circumstances, cover may include any of the previously mentioned objects or situations. But it is usually composed of such things as weed beds, lily pads, large rocks or boulders, deadfalls, undercut banks, plunge pools (those located beneath a waterfall), stumps, and many other things. Fish use cover for concealment and protection from predators or even the sun. Whereas both structure and cover attract fish, the former is usually associated with a holding or feeding station, for example, whereas the latter is always used for protection. Thus, in order to fulfill the need for shelter, bass always seek out those areas that provide adequate cover.

Undoubtedly, your favorite stream is inundated with

cover in one form or another. And although the shallow flat might hold a few weed beds, or a small log that could be used to conceal small fish, these objects would hardly suffice to hide a large fish from its predators. Consequently, a large fish would probably feel skittish in such an environment, unless it was night, when the fish could use darkness as cover. At any rate, this is why we don't often find large fish inhabiting shallow areas within a stream.

Large fish need deep water. In deep water, the water itself becomes cover for the bass. Add to this any number of objects, such as logs, rocks, boulders, and the like, and you get a fairly sheltered area. This is the second half of the equation. When you throw in a solid food supply, the bass have everything they need within one concentrated area, which they seldom have to leave. Such areas allow resident fish to grow old and large, because they are so well provided for. This is why the majority of the large fish within any given stream are caught from deep pools. They can eat, they can grow, they're protected, they can live in peace, and they don't have to leave home to do it.

Regardless of where it's located on a stream, find an area that provides food and shelter, and you'll find the bass.

Chapter 5

The Diet of Small-Stream Bass

*L*ARGEMOUTH, SMALLMOUTH, AND SPOTTED bass are remarkably adaptable creatures, able to survive and prosper on a highly varied diet, including everything from insects to amphibians, fishes to invertebrates, even reptiles and small mammals. This adaptability, along with bass's resilience to weather extremes and other adversities, account in no small part for their widespread distribution. And at no place is this adaptability better exercised and used than in the small stream.

A typical forage base for any given population of bass varies from one stream to the next and from one geographical area to another. This chapter will highlight some of the most common and widespread types. With the description of each particular forage item will be appropriate and suitable lure and fly imitations, which effectively mimic the natural prey.

INSECTS

Small streams, by their very nature, support enormous populations of insects, both aquatic and terrestrial. Some of these include stoneflies, mayflies, caddisflies, dragonflies, damselflies, moths, caterpillars, grasshoppers, and crickets. At certain times and places, all of these insects serve as food for bass, though they're most often associated with the trout's diet.

Some of these insects, such as the dragonfly, serve as bass forage in both their adult and nymph forms, whereas others seem to get the most attention after hatching. All three species of black bass feed on insects in part because they are so readily available in a stream environment. Some of the best areas to locate insects are over gravelly, muddy, or silty bottoms, often in fast water. Other good locations include those areas around weed beds, lily pads, and deadfalls. Small fish aren't the only ones that feed on insects—I have taken some hefty bass on both nymph and dry-fly patterns.

As you might expect, insects are best imitated with fly tackle. Insect patterns may be cast with lightweight rods and incite terrific action on the stream.

As far as fly patterns go, it is always best to study your stream in order to know what types of insects are present. Some of the most common are dragonflies, damselflies, moths, crickets, and grasshoppers, the adult forms of which may be effectively imitated with flies so designed to mimic the natural.

One of the best things that you can do is to buy a field guide listing common insects for your area. Then, using a fine-mesh net, collect samples of some of your stream's insect specimens and compare them with those depicted in the field guide. Once you've identified a few common species, exploit their presence with your flies.

A study in the art of opportunism, the black bass consumes a variety of forage, including insects, frogs, crayfish, small mammals, and other fishes.

Nymphs also make up an important part of the diet of stream bass, but unlike trout, you'll often have your best luck with larger patterns, such as size 8 or 10 stonefly or damselfly imitations. Of course, if your stream contains a good number of small fish and you're chasing them with a 3-weight fly-rod, by all means, feel free to use tiny patterns. But when large fish are present, you'll have your best luck with more substantial flies.

Another good species to imitate is the hellgrammite, one of the bass's favorite foods. When this insect is present in your stream, you can bet that it constitutes a serious portion of the bass's diet. There are several different fly patterns on the

76　　market tied to represent the natural hellgrammite, most of which work remarkably well. More recently, soft-plastic-lure manufacturers have begun offering hellgrammite molds for use with spinning tackle.

In any case, here's a final note about flies.

Nymphs are generally fished dead-drift or swing-drift style, usually beneath a strike indicator. And as is the case when trout fishing, presenting your imitation *drag free* is highly important. This goes for dry flies as well.

It is also a good idea to work nymph patterns along or just above the stream bottom, where the bass are accustomed to seeing the naturals. Although the use of insect-imitating flies is more commonly associated with trout fishing, don't exclude them from your fly box simply because they seem too dainty to take bass. Under the right conditions, nymphs, dry flies, and terrestrial patterns all work remarkably well. And when the bass are lethargic and inactive, a large nymph bumped along the bottom may just salvage your day.

FROGS

Frogs of various types and sizes are found in and around most streams in the United States. They constitute a favorite food for all species of black bass (especially the largemouth bass, which is more often found in shallow water, where frogs are found), as they are easy targets for the fish and provide a substantial meal. Frogs thrive around aquatic vegetation, such as weed beds, lily pads, and grass, and may frequently be seen jumping from a stream bank into the water as you walk the banks. Naturally, bass are accustomed to seeing frogs along the stream edges, where these amphibians feel more secure.

Tadpoles are also a delicacy of bass—especially large bass. A tadpole is the immature form of a frog, and these creatures are usually found in shallow, slower water within a stream. These areas are often located next to a bank, near a weed bed, or around similar structure, which they use as cover from predators.

Because tadpoles inhabit such shallow water, it stands to reason that bass feed most heavily on them early and late in the day, during periods of low light. At such times, bass frequently throw caution into the wind and move surprisingly shallow to feed on these nutritious creatures.

Frogs and tadpoles may be effectively imitated with both fly and conventional tackle. Surface poppers made of cork or foam are frequently used to imitate frogs, though there are also some excellent deer-hair patterns available. Divers are another logical option for mimicking frogs. There are also a handful of sculpin patterns on the market, which, perhaps inadvertently, effectively imitate tadpoles. If you tie your own flies, you may wish to use marabou in the tail, for this provides a tantalizing, undulating motion, highly indicative of the natural.

For those using conventional tackle, there are many frog patterns available, such as the Hula-Popper. There are also more than a few plastic frog imitations on the market today, most of which are designed to be weedless for working the areas in which frogs normally live. On some bass streams during spring and early summer, these plastic frogs are frequently worth *your* weight in gold!

Tadpoles may be imitated by using almost any soft-plastic or pork bait of a few inches in length, which incorporates a short, rounded body with an elongated, wavy tail. Sometimes you can modify one of these baits by cutting or trimming it until it suits you. To imitate a tadpole, fish your lure or fly near shallow, weedy areas, manipulating the offering with short, quick strips of the line while raising and lowering your rod's tip.

CRAYFISH

Crayfish are widely distributed throughout the United States and, when available, constitute a significant portion of the black bass's diet. If that's not enough for you to realize the importance of these invertebrates, then consider that crayfish are also one of the bass's *favorite* foods—the sight of one will almost always prompt a vicious strike.

Crayfish typically inhabit rocky and sometimes gravelly areas of a stream. In the South, you'll often find them in sections with mud bottoms, provided that there is also sufficient cover in the form of logs or large rocks. Crayfish, or "crawdads," as they are sometimes referred to, are highly active during low-light periods, which may be one reason why bass seem to feed so heavily on them, because it is during this time that the bass are normally most active. Under bright skies, crayfish normally hide under rocks and logs.

Crayfish are most active during the warmer months, but don't underestimate the effectiveness of such a lure or fly used during winter, especially in the South. Bass are accustomed to rooting and prying these morsels from their hiding places and think nothing of pouncing on one working its way across the stream bottom, even on the coldest days. In the South, the winter water temperature of many streams seldom dips below 50 degrees Fahrenheit. In these situations, crayfish can often be seen moving around on the stream bottom, though their movements are typically sluggish.

The great thing about using lures or flies that imitate crayfish is that you are almost guaranteed a bite, provided you manipulate the offering in a convincing manner. Thus, you should realize that these creatures inhabit the stream bottom and usually move about in a slow crawling motion. However, at the sight of a predator, they are capable of covering great distances rather quickly, always by moving in reverse. (If working a crayfish fly during winter, omit this part from your presentation.)

With conventional tackle, crayfish may be imitated with soft-plastic baits, such as tubes or even crayfish-specific molds. Jig-and-pork combinations also provide a tantalizing sight for bass, as do orange, red, tan, or brown crankbaits worked across the stream bottom.

For the fly-fisher, crayfish patterns are often tied to look remarkably similar to the natural. Some even go so far as to spray the fly with a crawfish scent, which is an ethical consideration among some fly-anglers. Whether you use a crayfish lure or fly, an important consideration is size. To that end, one of the best things you can do is examine the stream bottom, roll over logs and rocks, and find some crayfish. Not only will this allow you to duplicate their size, but also you'll know what color of offering to use. Given that more than 350 species of crayfish are found in North America, you may find yourself using orange, brown, olive, red, purple, or a variation of any of these colors in order to imitate the natural.

The important thing, however, is to get your fly to the bottom and work it in short strips. Take your time when using a crayfish pattern, and you will be rewarded.

SMALL FISHES

Small fishes—such as chubs, sculpins, darters, minnows, shiners, and sunfish—compose much of the bass's diet in small waters. The larger a bass grows, the more important are such fish to its diet. Any stream in which you find healthy populations of bass will likely also contain healthy and self-sustaining populations of baitfish.

A number of these forage fish are bottom dwellers, found near riffles and over rocky, gravely, or sandy bottoms. These include the mad toms and sculpins, along with several varieties of minnows, shiners, chubs, and daces. Darters also make up part of this list, and many subspecies of this fish inhabit extremely shallow water, perhaps only inches deep. This is one reason that darters are frequently found near pool tails and other skinny-water areas.

Grass beds, weed edges, and other areas of aquatic vegetation also constitute prime bait-fish habitat. These small fishes are attracted to these areas not only for the protection they afford from predators, but also for the multitude of insect life they contain.

Many species of the minnow family are very small in size, growing to little more than an inch, whereas others reach 5 or 6 inches or more. Almost all of them figure prominently into the diet of small-stream bass.

Sunfish are another common forage fish. These fish are often found in shallow, slower areas within a stream, often over muddy or silty bottoms.

Baitfish-imitating plugs, lures, and flies constitute perhaps the majority of all fishing tackle. There is such a staggering assortment of these lures that many anglers grow perplexed when attempting to choose just the right ones.

For anglers using conventional tackle, forage fish may be imitated with both lipped and lipless crankbaits, as well as stickbaits, spinnerbaits, or soft plastics. Most stickbaits are designed primarily for work either on or just below the surface, though some models work well down to several feet in the

Minnow imitations are a must on the small bass stream.

water column. Lipless crankbaits are generally excellent for use at middepths when open water is encountered and even work well when jigged vertically off the bottom. These baits are also great for quick retrieves when the fish are highly active.

Lipped crankbaits are very effective for working on or near the stream bottom, as the lip gives these lures not only an enticing action, but also some amount of snag resistance. Naturally, lipped crankbaits excel in horizontal presentations. And aside from imitating baitfish, these lures are also frequently used to mimic crayfish.

Anglers using fly tackle are also able to effectively imitate baitfish by using such patterns as the Clouser Deep Minnow and Lefty's Deceiver. Of course, there are a number of productive patterns on the market today, including many sculpin, shiner, and chub imitations. When attempting to imitate sculpins, which lack swim bladders, it is always a good idea to work your fly slowly across the stream bottom. Ditto for chubs, as this minnow prefers to hold near the bottom of broken-water areas. Shiner patterns are usually best used higher in the water column and especially around weed edges.

OTHER FOODS

There are always other creatures that are incidental to a bass's diet but are readily preyed upon in the right situation. These include mice, which occasionally fall into the water from trees or logs; small birds, which may become injured and fall into a stream; butterflies; snakes; lizards; salamanders; leeches, which when present in a stream are constantly preyed upon; and many other species.

The thing to remember about small-stream bass is that they are opportunists, and given the opportunity to take an easy meal, they will almost always do so. After all, their survival depends on it.

Chapter 6

Evaluating and Reading Small Streams

N OW THE FUN part begins. You get to determine
whether your potential stream is suitable for fishing
and catching quality black bass. There are many factors that, when working in concert, combine to make a good
stream. Yet, a single adverse characteristic might seriously degrade the stream and cause you to look elsewhere.

After you've determined the general location in which
you want to fish, bought a detailed map, studied the area, and
selected a few potential destinations, here's what you'll want
to look for when evaluating a particular stream's potential.

WATER QUALITY

The first thing I look at when examining any stream is the
water quality. Good water quality is imperative to a stream's
health and often determines the type of fish found there. It

84   should also tell you a good deal about the stream's sources and any potential detriments to its overall quality.

What is the color of the water? Is the water stained, murky, muddy, or relatively clear? The water in many of the streams I fish on the plains and in the Midwest bears a greenish tint, as do many of those in the East. This is a good sign because I know that such a stream is probably spring fed or fed by another spring-fed tributary. It also tells me that the bottom composition is largely rocky or gravelly, which is a characteristic I look for in most small streams. Rocks often ensure good insect and fish life. Additionally, they are an important part of the smallmouth bass's habitat, one of my favorite targets.

Not all streams will have water of this color. Some will run absolutely clear, whereas others may be dingy or worse.

In the latter case, you may try walking the stream bank and inspecting another location. Dirty water, although it can hold fish like largemouth bass, is often a detriment to a stream. And when you encounter such water, you're most likely to find other species, such as catfish or carp. These two are excellent targets for fly-rodders, but we're dealing with black bass here, so let's look for clean water.

It's important to note that water clarity will vary according to the time of year. For example, spring often finds even the clearest streams running high and dingy. Therefore, it would behoove you to examine your prospective streams during summer or winter, when conditions are usually more stable.

STRUCTURE

The next thing I look for in a good bass stream is structure. Are there any fallen logs—submerged or partially submerged? Any waterfalls, undercut banks, brushy banks, ledges, gravel bars, boulders, or mixed rock? If so, then the stream has one of the crucial elements for good bass water.

Weed beds, grass beds, and other aquatic vegetation such as lily pads are another good sign. These areas are home to a myriad of insect life, and they provide good cover for small fish and frogs, an important part of the bass's diet.

One of my favorite bass streams in northwest Arkansas possesses many such grass beds and weedy areas, which are located near the tails of its pools. These areas are often completely submerged during the high-water periods of spring, and then later only partially as the water level recedes in the summer and early fall. Nearly every year I take several quality bass by working these areas.

Of particular importance are the pools. Are they full of logs, rocks, boulders, weeds, brush, or other structure? If so, then chances are they hold some larger fish. In pools where structure is sparse, large fish may also be found, though there probably won't be as many, nor will they be as large as those found in pools with heavy structure.

THE STREAM ITSELF

You can determine a lot about a stream by studying its size, shape, flow, bottom composition, shorelines, and other factors. Examining the banks and perimeters of a stream will often tell you a great deal about those underwater characteristics that may be invisible to you above the surface. For a real eye opener, you may wish to put on a mask and snorkel the stream sometime when the weather is warm. Not only will such an experience reward you with the sight of many fish, you'll also see where these fish hide and what kind of structure and other features the stream contains.

Without snorkeling, however, you can look at the stream

banks. Are the banks heavily wooded? In the event that they are, you may notice some trees leaning over on the very edge of the stream bank, their roots exposed as a result of erosion, waiting their turn to fall into the water. If so, you can bet that the stream bottom contains its share of deadfalls, logs, and other woody debris. This is good.

What about the banks themselves? Are they tall, shallow, rocky, sandy, or muddy? Do they drop suddenly, or do they gradually taper into the water? Notice any ledges? If so, you can bet that the same sort of topography exists somewhere in the stream, and when you locate such an area, you will have found a hot spot.

Also, don't fail to look for any evidence of high water. Examine the banks, the trees, and the brush. Do you notice any high-water deposits, such as driftwood or other woody debris? Extremely high water can wreak havoc on a stream, displacing structure. But it can also open up the buffet table for the fish with the worms and insects it pulls into the stream from shore.

Finally, look to see whether the stream is running or stagnant. Running water is preferable, as it ensures a continuous supply of forage for the fish and cleaner, well-oxygenated water. Are there any large or deep pools? How about riffles or waterfalls? Healthy bass streams generally possess a pool/riffle/run sequence, which is further punctuated by flats 0and chutes, much like a trout stream. The more diverse a stream, generally the better the fishing.

FORAGE

Next, I look for signs of life, both in and out of the water. Do you notice schools of minnows, darters, or other baitfish? How about crayfish? When looking for a stream's forage content, it is always advisable to study several different areas within the stream. In other words, don't come up to a flat, give it a once-over, and then decide that no fish exist simply because you do not find any signs of life. Walk the bank, follow the stream, and check the next flat or pool. This task can be greatly facilitated with a pair of waders or hip boots, as you can do a more thorough examination.

You should also pay attention as you walk the banks. Do you notice any frogs jumping into the stream? How about grasshoppers or other insects? Should you notice anything flutter into the water as you pass, crouch down and wait to see if a fish comes up to eat the critter.

In the event you choose to evaluate a particular stream during inhospitable weather conditions, such as winter, realize that the fish are probably very lethargic and will be more difficult to find. But if they are present, you can usually determine so. If the weather has recently been very cold, perhaps below freezing for a few days, or if the water temperature has dropped below about 40 degrees Fahrenheit for several days, then carefully examine the banks below pools and riffles for any signs of dead baitfish. A severe cold front will often take its toll on these forage fish, which will be readily apparent in such locations. Some streams even smell fishy. Pay attention to what's going on around you, and you'll do fine.

ACCESSIBILITY

One feature of a stream that we often overlook is its accessibility. How easily can you get in and fish the stream? Are there shallow areas? Deep areas? Is the brush so heavy on the bank that you'll have a hard time getting to the water? Of course, another issue along this line is that of legal accessibility. Do you or can you obtain permission to fish the stream? Or, does the stream run through public land? Because we've covered

88   this issue in a previous chapter, we are now assuming that you do have legal access to fish your stream.

Bear in mind that some streams are wader friendly, whereas others may require the use of a small boat or float tube. Don't reject a stream simply because it looks inhospitable to wading. Rather, look for ways in which you can fish from the bank or from a boat. Many of the best locations on small streams go untouched simply because they are precarious to access.

FISHING PRESSURE

How much is your particular stream fished by other anglers? This is an easy thing to determine; all you have to do is consider how remote or convenient the stream is. This system isn't foolproof, but it gets you into the ballpark with some accuracy.

Is the stream located near a highway or other major road? If so, realize that it is subject to at least some pressure from other anglers, simply because of its visibility and convenience. But this isn't all bad. One stream in North Carolina in which I used to fish bisected a state highway and consequently was highly popular with local fishermen. I made dozens of trips to that stream and very often encountered other anglers. However, most of these anglers fished with night crawlers or some other form of live bait. In fact, anytime I queried area bait shops about what the fish were biting, the responses were almost always "night crawlers" and "shiners." I quickly realized that the fish, although they were pressured, weren't used to seeing such things as my flies. As a result, I took care to always fish the stream with fly tackle and usually caught quite a few fish.

Some of the best streams are located in relatively undeveloped or uninhabited areas. These often take some time to locate, but when you do find one, make the effort to examine it thoroughly. If access to the stream appears to be gained only through hiking in, chances are that you've found a place that receives relatively little fishing pressure.

Another excellent place to look for suitable bass streams is on public hunting land; those who use such land are almost always there to hunt, not fish.

You can also tell a great deal about a stream's fishing pressure simply by studying the banks. Do you notice any trash lying on the ground? Any footprints or well-worn trails leading to the water? If so, this might be cause for you to look for another stream, or at least another area on the same stream.

As a rule of thumb, the more distant a stream is located from roads, houses, highways, parking lots, and other development, generally the better the fishing will be. We are creatures of comfort and convenience, and relatively few of us take the time or make the effort to go out of our way in locating a fishing hole, especially when more convenient ones exist.

STOCKING

Many small streams are regularly stocked by state fish and game departments, whereas others receive absolutely no support. If your stream is one of the latter, and holds fish, then rest assured that they are wild or native to that stream. This is very often the case with remote and out-of-the-way waters, those far from any large cities or suburbs.

Stocked streams, on the other hand, generally present some sort of deficiency, which prevents them from sustaining strong populations of fish. In some cases, a stream's only apparent deficiency may be too many anglers. Others suffer from

Small-stream bass are occasionally the products of state-managed stockings. More often, however, they are wild creatures, indigenous to that stream.

poor water quality, inadequate forage, and similar maladies.

You can usually obtain a list of state-stocked streams by writing your state fish and game department. Be advised, however, that these streams are generally well publicized as such and, consequently, are popular with other anglers.

Of course, there is frequently the issue of escapee fish, which are stocked in one water only to emigrate and invade another, but this is a different subject entirely. Just remember that if you're looking for that overlooked or forgotten stream, chances are you aren't looking for the stocked stream.

READING THE WATER

Now we'll assume that you've assessed your particular stream and found it worthy of your time and effort. Let's explore the different parts of a typical stream and find out how to best fish these areas.

Tributary Streams

Tributaries, often called feeder creeks, do many things for a small stream. They provide a stream with additional water, current, forage, cover, and many other things. Thus, tributaries increase options for bass. Naturally, the more of these options a given section of stream contains, the more desirable such an area is to bass. While small streams themselves are sometimes tributaries for larger rivers or lakes, very often they are also the beneficiaries of such a relationship. Any time you encounter a tributary it is deserving of your time and attention, for they always attract bass.

Because stream-run bass instinctively face into the current, it stands to reason that you'll almost always find them holding below the tributary. Obviously, this affords bass the opportunity to intercept any baitfish coming down with the

92   main flow, as well as those being discharged from the feeder stream.

But baitfish aren't the only forage product of tributaries. Crayfish are common, especially in rocky areas. Insects and microscopic plankton are also fed into the main stream via these flowing conveyor belts. This, in turn, attracts minnows, shiners, and other baitfish, which feed upon these morsels. Naturally, predators like bass aren't far behind.

Depending on its own sources, water volume, the time of year, and other factors, a tributary can also attract bass for the oxygenated water it delivers to the stream. This can be terribly important during summer, when a stream's water temperatures rise and the amount of dissolved oxygen declines. The small-mouth bass, in particular, is attracted to those areas featuring a current and oxygenated water.

Tributaries also provide additional cover for stream bass. For example, if a tributary's banks are sandy or void of vegetation, you can expect that the water it discharges into the main stream during periods of high water will be correspondingly silty or turbid. The greater a tributary's inherent characteristics differ from those of the main stream, the more dramatic the effect will be on the stream and its bass.

Let's say the banks of your home stream are heavily vegetated with trees, grass, and other plants. This would constitute healthy riparian habitat, which helps limit erosion, runoff, and such. Consequently, the water in your stream likely remains clearer as a result.

However, let's say that one of your stream's tributaries runs through a section of cleared farmland on its course to the confluence with the main stream. In this case it is quite likely that most any moderate rain shower would wash a good deal of soil and silt into the water, which would soon find its way into the main stream. As this muddy water enters the clear, main

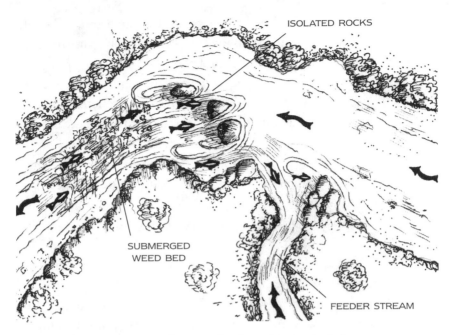

ISOLATED ROCKS

SUBMERGED
WEED BED

FEEDER STREAM

In those areas where a tributary feeds a stream, look for
bass around the confluence and just downstream, where
they will hold near any available cover, such as weed beds
or rocks.

stream, it tends to cloud it up. The main current carries some
of this sediment away, though it forces much of it to either
side. The result is the formation of a mudline.

Mudlines are nothing more than confined clouds of sediment in the water. While they eventually dissipate as the current carries away the debris, they are hotspots for bass while
they remain.

Largemouth, smallmouth, and spotted bass use mudlines
as cover from which to ambush their prey. And because bass
feel less exposed while in mudlines, they concentrate heavily
in these areas, even when they're located in shallow water.
In some cases, however, the situation is reversed. Sometimes
the main flow is dingy or turbid, while the tributary dispenses

clear water. Mudlines also occur in this situation, although they tend to be more confined. Nevertheless, bass use them to their advantage, and so should you.

Tributaries often feed a stream with water that is warmer or cooler than its own. Of course, this can be determined by carrying a stream thermometer and using it to take water-temperature readings up in the tributary, and in the main stream, above and below the confluence. If the tributary is fed by a spring, then there is a good chance that its water temperature will differ from that of the main stream during summer and winter. This factor alone would serve to attract fish during these times.

Yet another important factor about tributaries is that they frequently produce eddies, seams, and other features as they merge with the main current. The most dramatic and important of these features, regardless of what they are, are almost always located just below the tributary's confluence with the main stream, and to either side. Find a piece of cover in one of these areas, such as a log or boulder, and chances are that you've found a prime feeding station for big bass.

As you can see, tributaries greatly enhance a stream's potential. Though some feeder streams are themselves sufficiently large for holding bass, more often they simply enhance the main stream by increasing its diversity. In most cases, the key points are a tributary's confluence with the main stream, and the area immediately below.

When targeting these locations, key on the current seams, deep pockets or chutes, eddies, boulders, logs, piles of rocks, weedbeds, shaded areas, and undercut banks. Once again, the more of these features a confluence area contains, the more desirable is the location to bass.

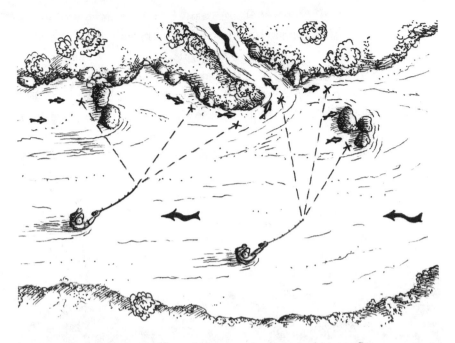

In a small stream environment, bass are attracted to confluences with feeder creeks. To effectively work such an area,
the angler should position himself across from the tributary
and fish the opposite side of the stream with a series of fan
casts.

Riffles

Riffle areas are usually quite shallow, though sometimes they
may run to a few feet deep. They consist of a moderate to fast
current flowing over small- to medium-sized rocks. The water
here is well oxygenated, and these areas are favorite haunts of
bass at certain times of the day and year.

Riffles are quite often home to large numbers of insects
and sometimes hold minnows and other baitfish. Yet, because
of the shallow nature of riffles, bass tend to occupy these areas
primarily during times of low light. One exception to this is

96   where a riffle area spills into a pool, or where it contains a cut
or a ledge. These features indicate the presence of deeper
water, and whenever bass have the opportunity to take a deep-
water highway up into a riffle area to feed, look out. They can
be productive at any time of the day.

In any case, just as the fast water affords the fish a certain
amount of overhead cover, so too does it help you in masking
your movements. Consequently, you can often wade in fairly
close in order to make your cast.

For fly-anglers, such areas are generally best fished by
casting upstream and drifting nymph or streamer patterns
through the target area. Another effective technique is to position yourself on either side of the stream and cast a streamer
pattern perpendicular to the current. Pay special attention to

When quietly waded, riffles can help mask your approach.

In swifter water, a reach cast will allow you to get your streamer fly or nymph deeper before the current has a chance to pull it away.

those areas containing any noticeable current breaks, such as boulders, and strive to present your fly into these areas. If these likely spots fail to produce, you can usually count on taking a good fish from the point where a riffle enters a pool.

Fly anglers can also cast their offerings down-and-across stream, allowing the current to carry the fly downstream. This is effective with both minnow and crayfish patterns.

Anglers using conventional tackle can often have success by working the water in a similar manner and casting small crankbaits or jerkbaits. If up- and across-stream presentations fail to produce, don't be afraid of tossing your lure out and allowing the current to sweep it downstream. Just as the lure begins to swing back your way, begin an erratic retrieve by jerking your rod tip, reeling, and pausing. Line control should be no problem here, as working your lure back against the current will keep the line tight.

Flats

Flats may be defined as shallow areas, often from 1 to 3 feet deep, which feature relatively smooth and uniform bottoms. Currents moving through such areas are often slow to moderate; consequently, bass holding in flats tend to be quite spooky. Flats may also feature sand, mud, or even gravel bottoms, many times with heavy wood or rock structure. These areas tend to hold good numbers of sunfish, minnows, tadpoles, frogs, insects, and crayfish.

Because flats are shallow and relatively calm, they are best fished from either downstream or from the bank. When working from the bank, take care to keep a low profile, wear drab-colored clothes, and try to keep trees, brush, or any other streamside cover at your back, so as to break up your silhouette.

Flats lend themselves to streamer patterns, such as minnow imitations or woolly buggers. These flies may be effectively fished with up- or across-stream casts and worked with a short stripping motion. Sometimes poppers are beneficial for surface work, particularly early or late in the day when fished near the bank or over logs. Because fish holding on flats can be quite skittish, it is best to try a softer popper first, such as deer-hair model. These flies don't produce as much noise as the hard-bodied models and, consequently, are less likely to spook fish. If this fails to produce but a top-water offering still has your confidence, then go with a hard cork or foam popper.

When using conventional tackle, try a small floating jerkbait or crankbait, worked across stream. Long casts are frequently required in order to avoid spooking the fish. This is one instance when an ultralight spinning outfit really shines, provided that there isn't too much heavy cover. When stumps, logs, or deadfalls are present, necessitating heavier line, use a casting outfit and work a weedless jig, plastic worm, or tube slowly across the bottom.

Gravel Bars

Most small streams possess gravel bars, though sometimes these features are composed of sand or even mud. Gravel bars are typically home to large numbers of baitfish, such as minnows, shiners, and sometimes darters. Naturally, you should strive to imitate such forage when working these features.

I find that gravel bars are best targeted by working them from the downstream side, though at times you may be able to position yourself parallel to the feature and work the area from across the stream. Gravel bars are usually most productive early and late in the day, and especially at night.

Regardless of the type of tackle you use, minnow- or other baitfish-imitating offerings are your best bet when working these areas. It is important to experiment with different retrieves until you find the one that works best for any given day. Sometimes, a steady, quick retrieve will do the trick, though when the fish are finicky, you may find that slower lure movement, combined with intermittent pauses, works better.

When working gravel bars, always make sure to cover the very end or tip of the feature, where it meets deeper water. If a large rock, log, or channel is evident near the area, take your time and thoroughly cover the location before moving on. Such a situation fairly well spells B-A-S-S!

Gravel bars are the scenes of frequent run-and-gun-style assaults by bass on their hapless bait-fish victims. These brief, sporadic episodes typically occur early or late in the day, but they may also take place during the middle of the day, especially during spring or fall. Obviously, the bass are attracted by the baitfish, but because these areas are shallow, the savvy predators avoid loitering any longer than necessary. Quite often, the bass will take up nearby stations at any log, boulder, or ledge in the vicinity.

For this reason, it is advisable to carefully work the areas surrounding gravel bars, as well as the bars themselves. This may entail the productive water 20 yards or so downstream from the feature or perhaps a ledge just upstream. If a gravel bar holds any baitfish, and most of them do, then chances are the bass won't be far away.

Chutes and Runs

Chutes and runs, as they are frequently known, are moderately deep areas, often 2 to 4 feet. These areas are frequently found in or below riffles, connecting them with flats or sometimes pools. They are transition zones between shallow and deeper water and serve as highways and thoroughfares for the fish. Quite often they bear swift to moderate currents and mark the presence of a channel or ditch, which offers the fish something of a sanctuary for moving up and down a stream.

As you may have guessed, chutes and runs can hold fish at any time of the day or night, though they are usually most productive at dawn and dusk. It is during these times that large bass are most likely to be found here, almost always near any available cover. Whenever you encounter one of these features, don't ever pass up the opportunity to fish it.

One reason these areas are so productive is that they concentrate the fish to a relatively confined location. Although chutes and runs may be relatively short or long, sometimes running 40 or 50 feet in length, they are generally quite narrow and confined. Fish use them because they funnel forage, making them good feeding stations while also offering some degree of cover with slightly deeper, and often running, water.

The best way to fish a chute or run is to approach the feature from downstream and to one side. Make long casts, and maintain contact with your fly or lure. Experiment by working your offering high in the water column, then middepth; if that fails, drag it across bottom. Sometimes, the fish may be positioned directly on bottom, especially when the chute or run contains logs, large rocks, or other structure that breaks the current and offers the bass a good lie. Other times, however, the fish hold to one side, right on the break.

Some of the best areas are those where the chute enters or exits a pool, marking a transition area that concentrates the current and forage. In any case, make sure to thoroughly saturate these areas while slowly working your way upstream.

Pools

Pools are one of my favorite places to fish on a stream because they always hold bass—and very often large ones. By now you recognize the importance of a pool to a fish's need for food and shelter. Usually, they provide both. This is why you find so many fish holding in these areas, whether they are small or large pools.

Pools feature a slower current, generally because they open up and expand the boundaries of a stream for a certain distance. Often positioned below riffles, a flat, a chute, or a run, pools mark transition points between areas of faster water. Because of their increased dimensions, the water has someplace to go, whether down or out, which slows the current. As the water filters through the pool, it gains speed near the tail before spilling over a falls, through a riffle, or into a chute or run.

Pools are almost always best fished by working upstream. There's a reason for this. Fish instinctively face into the current (not necessarily upstream, but always into the current),

Some of the best places to find bass in a small stream are
structure-choked pools.

which is where they expect to receive their food. Fishing a pool from the downstream or down-current side, and thus working upstream, helps avoid spooking the fish, which would otherwise see your approach. Often, however, a pool will be so long or deep that you can't effectively cover the entire area by wading in from downstream. In this case, it is often advantageous to get out of the stream and approach the pool from either side on the bank. When a certain situation necessitates fishing from the bank, strive to maintain a low profile and keep your movements to a minimum. Fish can often see surprisingly well in a pool because of the clear water and reduced current.

In any pool, there are certain places that are almost always more productive than others: the head, tail, and the major structural feature. Though bass may be caught from almost any point within, concentrating on these three areas dramatically increases your chances at a big fish.

The head of a pool usually receives its water from riffles, a waterfall, a chute, or a run. In such cases, the current at the pool's head will be noticeably faster than surrounding areas as it spills in. Fish know that this current brings with it food in the form of insects, crayfish, minnows, and such. Naturally, the bass will often station themselves at the head of the pool, right where the current and their food supply enters. Sometimes, you may find the fish directly beneath a waterfall or below and to either side of the entering current. Other times the predators station themselves a few feet or yards downstream, beside a log or rock. Take the time to target these areas carefully, fishing from the top of the water column to the bottom.

The tail receives the water that has flowed through the pool and is preparing to exit the same via a waterfall, chute, run, or some other feature. Because a pool's lower boundary is defined by some feature that concentrates and funnels the

104   water—thereby marking the end of the pool and the beginning of the next stream feature—the current here picks up
some steam before exiting. Inasmuch as the water and current
are more confined at the tail of a pool, it follows that bass will
relate heavily to these areas, just as they do with the pool's
head. The tail of a pool offers the fish a good opportunity at
nabbing any sort of forage that has drifted through the area
and is preparing to leave and wash downstream. This concen-
tration of water and forage is what makes the tail so important.

The major structural feature within a pool may be a
boulder, a large log, deadfall, brush pile, ledge, depression, or
almost any other feature that would serve to attract fish. Fish
instinctively know which piece of structure within any given
area affords the best opportunities for food and cover. These
choice spots are almost always taken by the largest fish. Therefore, by concentrating on such structure, which is often located
in or near the deepest part of the pool, you can consistently
catch quality fish, provided you do everything else right.

Although any section of stream can hold fish at certain
times of the day or year, pools hold the most and largest fish
and therefore should receive the majority of your attention.

Eddies and Seams

Eddies—sometimes called "back eddies"—and seams attract
bass at all times of the day and night. The former feature may
be likened to a blender, which pulls in food from the nearby
current and blends it into one condensed vortexlike area.
Seams, then, are proverbial rest stops along the highway of the
current, where predators like bass can simply take a breather
while waiting for the one-way current to deliver the food.

Eddies and seams are often found beside chutes and runs,
below riffles and pools, or sometimes within the pools themselves. Both mark current variances within the stream: Eddies

spin back and around from the main current, whereas seams are simply identified by slower water abutting a faster current. In a stream, all predator fish use the current to their advantage as it delivers a constant supply of food. Bass simply hold in protected areas just off the current, where they can intercept their prey.

If your objective in coming to the small stream is indeed to catch bass, then under no circumstances should you ever pass up an eddy or good-looking seam. They always hold fish.

Some eddies are large (often 4 to 8 feet in diameter), whereas some are like miniature tornadoes (only 12 inches or so). Sometimes, they occur in open water, next to a flat; other times they are found beneath overhanging bushes or trees, beside a steep bank. Regardless of where you find one, pitch a lure into it. Bait-fish imitations are generally the best choice, though almost anything will work in an eddy.

Like eddies, seams can be highly productive, provided you don't overlook them. To find them, simply look for those areas where a fast current meets a slower one. Sometimes, seams are found directly below or beside eddies.

Generally, the most productive part of a seam is the exact point where the faster current meets the slower one. Other times, the sweet spot is well off the main current, almost always in the slower water. As with anything else in life, experiment until you find what works.

Ledges

Ledges constitute another of my favorite stream features, for they are logical places to find bass, especially large ones. Sometimes, you can easily spot a ledge from above the surface; other times they are located in deeper or swifter water and can be discerned only by means of some careful wading, or snorkeling, if you're so inclined.

Anytime I encounter a ledge, seeing the shallow water on one side and the deeper, dark, and mysterious water on the other, my pulse goes into high gear. Immediately, I am wound tighter than a three-day clock, but things appear to be moving in slow motion. I am simply unable to move quickly enough to get my lure into the water. But that's just what I strive to do, as quickly as possible, because I know that I'm going to catch a fish.

Is this psychological wherewithal somehow a testament to my confidence? Sometimes. More often, however, it is evidence supporting the productivity of ledges.

Ledges are usually composed of rock, slate, or some other hard surface and offer bass comfortable lies and natural ambushing spots. A mild drop of no more than 6 or 10 inches may constitute some ledges, whereas others may plummet 4 or 5 feet in depth. In any case, ledges—and especially ledges that afford some sort of overhead cover—attract bass.

There are times and certain situations in which fishing a ledge can be difficult. Often, ledges are found in heavy- or fast-flowing areas, which means that you may have trouble getting a lure down to the fish. On the flip side, fish holding on ledges tend to be less spooky, because they feel less exposed and more secure. This means that you can often approach a ledge, and its fish, much more closely than those found on a shallow flat. Of course, it helps to avoid kicking rocks or stumbling and falling into the water.

The trick is to get your lure down to the fish and into their strike zone. This means that if you put your lure down at the fish's depth, but it's 3 feet outside of their holding position, you're quite likely to get no strikes. Instead, put your lure right in front of the fish so that it has no choice but to strike.

For fly-anglers, this may entail using long leaders, extra split shot, sinking-tip lines, and certainly long casts well upstream of the target area. In other words, put something weighty on and give it time to sink to the desired depth. As the current is usually sufficient to carry your lure back toward you, you can often fish the fly dead-drift style, even if you're using larger streamers.

If this fails, try repositioning yourself upstream of the ledge and off to one side or the other. That's right: *upstream* of the ledge and to one side. Just remember to avoid stirring up debris in the water. In other words, don't cross the stream; instead, stay on one side or the other. This way you won't disturb the fish.

Then, with the same sort of rig, cast well upstream of the ledge (even though you are standing upstream of the ledge) and give your fly time to sink as it approaches the target area. This may entail a simple roll cast out toward your side, or if the water is extremely deep, you may want to cast well upstream of your position so the fly will be nice and deep as it passes you on its way to the hot spot.

At any rate, line control is critical. You will probably want to use a strike indicator, and maybe two, if the current is sufficiently heavy. The idea here is to have the fly tumble off the ledge, right down to where the fish are holding. By standing upstream from the ledge, the current will actually help keep your line tight, which will facilitate strike detection. And because fish holding on a ledge generally have small strike zones (the current flowing over a ledge ensures a continuous and convenient supply of food, so the fish won't move far to eat), you will need to keep your fly as close to the magic window as possible for as long as possible. Your position upstream also helps accomplish this feat. Of course, your efforts are certainly enhanced by a quick, upstream mend or two, and sometimes by "high-sticking," whereby you keep as much line as possible off the water. This way, with only the leader penetrating the water, your fly isn't as easily distracted by the current, and it has a chance to reach deeper water.

This is an excellent technique for catching large bass, for these fish typically haunt such locations. If the current is heavy and the fish fairly large, prepare yourself for a savage battle—one you won't soon forget.

When using casting or spinning tackle, you can often get by without putting the lure directly down to the fish. This is because conventional lures are usually larger, bulkier, flashier, and noisier. In other words, the bass can detect these lures much easier than a fly. With conventional tackle, you can work upstream or downstream, and even across stream. The trick is to get your lure into the general vicinity, then use an erratic retrieve to seal the deal. I've had bass come up from 5 feet and more to take what they thought was a crazed and injured minnow.

Sometimes, bass are so perfectly placed and protected because their ledge affords them overhead cover. These are the most difficult bass to catch because it's highly arduous to get your lure down to where they can even see it. But we have a few remedies, including both an upstream and downstream approach.

In either event, use a heavy weedless jig with a pork trailer. The heavier the current and the deeper the water, the heavier your jig should be, and the smaller the trailer. The trick is to get your lure down quickly, where you can then drag it off the ledge; by virtue of its weight, the lure should quickly fall to the bottom, right in front of the fish, or at least where they can see it.

Sometimes, an upstream approach is best, as you can allow the current to carry your lure down to the ledge. Then, with a tight line, you can control the lure's fall. When you do it right, watch out!

There you have it. You now know how to evaluate a potential small stream, read its water, identify its various features, and rate its potential productivity. At last, we now get to go fishing. To that end, the next few chapters are dedicated to helping you make the most of your time on the water.

Chapter 7

Shallow-Water Tactics

MOST CREEKS AND STREAMS have more shallow than deeper water. Shallow water may be found in chutes or runs, on flats, and along the shorelines. It may hold riffles, eddies, or seams. In some cases, a pool may hold shallow water, but as previously mentioned, this is all relative.

Here, we'll assume that you've located a nice clear-running freestone stream that flows through the rolling countryside somewhere in your vicinity. Let's also assume that this stream is spring fed, thereby guaranteeing it a constant source of water. Certainly there are many flats, riffles, chutes, runs, and pools, some of which may exceed 5 feet in depth. So, given the availability of this deeper water, we'll then classify shallow water as that which is 2 to 3 feet or less at normal water levels, regardless of where it is found on the stream.

At some point during the course of history, a wise man (or maybe it was a woman) once said that 90 percent of the fish are found in 10 percent of the water. How insightful this person must have been, for it is accurate. This old adage applies not only to small streams, but to rivers, lakes, and reservoirs as well. But we're talking small streams here, so forget the other venues. Within our beloved little creeks and streams, 90 percent of the fish are found in 10 percent of the water, the 10 percent, of course, being the pools. But this can and does vary.

Certainly, pools hold most of the fish within a stream, especially the larger ones. But stream fish, like those found elsewhere, are migratory. Thus, a pool's fish population is given to fluctuation according to the time of year and even the time of day. And it is these fluctuations that we're concerned with here in our discussion of shallow water because such areas can and do hold fish. The wise man or woman was indeed onto something, but the numbers aren't entirely correct. For sometimes, shallow areas, which might compose 60 percent of a stream, hold 40 percent of the fish. Other times, they hold only 5 percent, but there are almost always fish present in shallow water. But perhaps this sage didn't notice them.

Some fish, like certain darters, for example, may spend their entire lives in shallow water, but other fish are seldom found here. Some spend only a part of their lives in the shallows. Baby bass spend much of their early lives in these areas, often near the bank. Here they relate to weed growth and other aquatic vegetation for protection from predators. These locations are also rich in insect life, on which young black bass feed. For these reasons, such areas are often referred to as *nursery water*.

On the other hand, mature bass tend to occupy shallow areas for one of two reasons: spawning or feeding. The former takes place in the spring, when water temperatures warm into the 60-degree Fahrenheit range. Of course, this varies according to location; spawning may occur as early as February in the South and as late as June in the North. Although not all fish within any given habitat spawn at exactly the same time, spawning is, nevertheless, a brief ritual. Once completed, the fish move back to deeper water.

Black bass also invade shallow water to feed. This is an inherently risky proposition, one of which the bass are instinctively aware, but also a rewarding opportunity to stock up on high-protein groceries. As mentioned in an earlier chapter, bass have many predators, such as raptors, otters, raccoons, and other species. It is primarily for this reason that the fish most frequently inhabit the shallows during periods of low light: mornings, evenings, and at night. This low light provides the fish with a certain amount of cover, under which they feel reasonably safe from their predators. These periods also afford the bass a better chance at ambushing their prey, as their eyesight under such conditions is generally superior to that of baitfish.

Like their lake- and reservoir-dwelling cousins, the feeding activity of stream-run bass is governed by many variables, including moon phase, barometric pressure, time of day, time of year, water temperature, and many others. At times, bass may feed heavily for a period of only fifteen or twenty minutes; other times, conditions may warrant a major feeding period of several hours or more. Regardless of the duration of such activity, however, bass inhabiting shallow water for purposes of feeding usually occupy such areas only for brief periods. When a bass retires to the safety of deep water after feeding, there may be several factors urging it to do so, but one of the foremost is its perceived exposure to predators. This threat remains with a bass throughout its life, governing its behavior from the time it hatches until it expires.

Now that you know something about why bass inhabit

shallow water, let's dissect those areas in our hypothetical stream and learn how to effectively fish them.

RIFFLES

The nice thing about riffles is that they attract fish. In fact, you can often pinpoint exactly where the fish will be early and late in the day, and at certain times of the year, simply by noting the locations of any riffle areas on your stream.

By their very nature, riffles are shallow areas, often only inches deep. In some cases, however, they may hold several feet of water. Generally speaking, the deeper the water, the more likely is the riffle to hold larger fish, and the more likely it is to hold fish throughout the day.

Bass gravitate to riffles because they are rich in insect life, and very frequently they harbor baitfish and other forage. This abundance of food, combined with the overhead cover of running water, make them logical feeding stations for bass. Smallmouth bass, in particular, are fond of riffles, though all species will use them when available. Just remember that whenever you find bass in riffles, you can bet that they are feeding. Consequently, these fish are excellent targets.

Another characteristic of riffles is that they provide highly oxygenated water. This is especially important during the summer, when a stream's water temperature may climb into the mid- to upper 80s. Heat and reduced amounts of dissolved oxygen stress fish, but they cope with these adversities by moving into riffles or below waterfalls, where they have a reasonable amount of cover, a constant supply of food, and greater dissolved oxygen. Given this, riffles become even more important to the angler working a stream during the summer.

Fly-fishers know that riffles are usually best fished from downstream. That is because you can approach the fish quite

RIPRAP/ ROCKS

RIFFLES

PENINSULA

Riffles attract bass for the plethora of forage they contain. Where they're joined by a peninsula, deep water, or rocks, they can hold fish any time of day.

closely (the noise and movement of the running water acts as both cover and distraction), cast upstream, and allow your fly to drift down with the current. This, of course, presents the offering in a natural manner, as the fish would normally see it. Aside from nymphs, some of the most effective flies are streamer patterns, such as woolly buggers or small minnow imitations. Here it is advisable to make short casts, which helps you to maintain contact with your fly. Shorter casts also mean less line on the water, which might otherwise interfere with your drift or ability to detect a strike.

Strike indicators are usually optional, but they may be absolutely necessary in particularly fast or rough riffles. Sometimes, two or even three indicators are required to effectively fish an area.

Another good way to fish riffles is to use an across-current approach. This technique is popular with anglers who use spinning or casting tackle, as it allows for a slower and more subtle presentation, thereby keeping the lure in front of the fish for a longer period of time. Sometimes, this is the key to getting bitten.

Fly-fishers can also benefit from an across-current approach, particularly in those areas where riffles flow into a pool, where deep water and large rocks and boulders are often found. Bait-fish imitations are logical choices for this sort of a situation because the fish holding in this type of water are often larger specimens looking for exactly this type of forage.

Some of the best lures for fishing riffles are small jerkbaits. These baits may be cast perpendicular to the current and retrieved erratically. Sometimes, it may be necessary to stand on one side of the target area and make an across- and slightly downstream cast at a 45-degree angle to the current. Then, with your line tight, slowly work the lure back, pausing frequently. Often, the strike will come just after the pause, as the lure begins moving forward.

There are times when fishing upstream of the riffles may be necessary because of heavy shoreline cover and the like. Such a technique isn't usually as effective as fishing from the downstream side, because the angler is apt to kick up dirt or silt and probably alert the fish. When conditions warrant, however, or when you've exhausted all other possibilities, move up to the head of the riffle via the shoreline if at all possible. Once in position, stand off to one side or the other; don't stand in the middle of the stream and try to work your lure down, as this may alert the fish. It is much tougher to work a riffle in this manner because the fish are more likely to spot you. This method can work, however, if you use a stealthy approach.

FLATS

Flats are terrific locations for catching bass at certain times of the day. Usually, the best times are mornings, evenings, and again at night. Night fishing will be covered in a later chapter, so here we'll concentrate on mornings and evenings.

The characteristics of any given flat differ from one to the next and from stream to stream, but often such areas are loaded with weed growth, grass beds, lily pads, and other aquatic vegetation. As mentioned earlier, this vegetation harbors insects, which attracts baitfish and frogs, both for its forage and cover. Consequently, predators like bass are attracted to such areas for the forage availability.

Some of the other characteristics of a flat may include a mud, sand, rock, or gravel bottom; wood structure; grassy shorelines; shoreline trees; and an abutting pool, riffle, run, chute, or bend. The more of this, the better, though almost all flats will hold bass at certain times.

I used to believe that truly large bass would move up onto a flat only during periods of low light. Although this is indeed the best time to find them, this isn't always the case. Several years ago I spent a week fishing a certain northwest Arkansas stream, which is known for both the size and numbers of its smallmouth bass. As it was mid-July and the afternoons terribly hot, I tended to fish early and late, and used the afternoons to rest in my motel room. Returning from lunch one afternoon, I passed over the stream on the way back to my room. Curious to see the stream from a different angle, I stopped my pickup alongside the road and went over to the bridge to have a look. I almost fell in!

Below the bridge was a flat with not more than 2 feet of water, on which I had taken a few bass the previous morning, but not much else. I assumed that it was too shallow, too open

Working the water from shore, before wading into the stream, will catch you more bass.

and exposed to hold fish during the middle of the day. Boy, was I wrong.

Below me, in the water, I counted more than a dozen bass ranging in size from 10 or 12 inches to more than 20 inches! The largest bass looked like it might weigh 5 pounds, certainly an exceptional small-stream specimen. I studied the fish for some time, watching in awe as the largest fish—the giant, 5-pound bronzeback—moved about leisurely and undisturbed. These fish were more or less exposed, at least from my point of view, but I didn't fail to notice the common denominator among all of them: They all remained in or very near a shadow. I knew that shadows were important, but this lesson served to remind me of just how important they really are. Then the next thing hit me.

Standing on the bridge, I looked up and down the stream and could see no one. In fact, I gathered that there had been no other anglers here all day, and since I had left for lunch the stream had been left unmolested. The fish knew when it was safe to come out.

Thus, I learned two things that day: first, that shallow water can hold fish, even during the middle of a hot sunny day, provided that suitable cover is available; second, that slipping in among these stream residents, undetected, is paramount if one is to have any hope of catching them.

Undoubtedly, stream bass are highly astute creatures. They have a knack for knowing exactly what is going on around them. Think that highly pressured streams don't hold many fish? Guess again. I have seen fish, both large and small, come out onto the playground after recess had ended for the anglers only too many times to think otherwise. They learn to adapt; they *have to* adapt in order to survive.

With this stark realization, I returned to the stream early that afternoon and proceeded to catch four bass off the flat, including a feisty 16-inch smallie. Since then I've learned a few things about fishing flats, which I'll share with you now.

Because we now know that flats can hold fish at any time of day, we should realize that we can catch them if only we can present our offering without alerting the fish to our presence. To that end, the greatest and most valuable tool an angler has in his or her possession is not a fancy rod or reel or any other tackle; it is *stealth*. This tool will catch you many more fish than all of the state-of-the-art tackle you own. Here's how we use it.

First of all, it helps to wear drab-colored clothing. You don't have to go so far as camouflage battle fatigues, but this doesn't hurt. Try to blend into the environment so that the fish can't see you. Always make an effort to wear something that is similar in color to the shoreline trees, brush, grass, and such. You may have a favorite bright-yellow fishing cap, but all the camouflage or drab clothing in the world won't do you any good if you wear that cap. The fish can spot such an object from a considerable distance. Thus, we need to outfit ourselves with dull- and natural-colored hats, vests, shirts, waders, and, during winter, gloves and coats.

The practice of blending into a stream environment for fishing is no different than hunting deer with archery equipment. In order to get a shot at your quarry, you have to thoroughly blend into your surroundings. You have to become the trees and shrubbery; you can't stand out. Otherwise, the fish or animal may never present itself within range. Be selective about what you wear to the stream, and be thorough in your approach to concealment.

Once you have this facet covered, let's move up to the stream.

Unless forced to fish from upstream, always approach the water you intend to fish from the downstream side. Also, don't just blunder up to the water's edge; stay back, crouch down, and try to keep some sort of cover between you and the water. Be patient. Kneel down, observe the stream, and find out what's going on. Are the fish feeding? Are they holding in the middle, or do you notice anything along the banks? What you observe here can tell you much about what the fish are doing, and it should also tell you what sort of offering and presentation will work best at that time. Remember, we have the entire flat to fish, so what you observe here at the tail of the flat should tell you a good deal about what's happening farther upstream.

Do you see any emergent vegetation? Any shoots or weeds? If so, study them. Study them *hard*. Fish holding among this sort of cover will often reveal themselves with their movement, which causes the vegetation around them to move. If the wind is blowing or if the current is running fast, this may not be readily apparent. But if all is still, except for an isolated area of movement here and there, that should tell you something. And if the weather is hot and the sun high in the sky, these areas should be among the first places you look.

Listening to what is going on around you can also tip you off as to what the fish are doing. Obviously, if you're near a riffle, falls, or other area of heavy current, this might not be possible. But on a flat, where the water is generally calm and still, a bass busting a minnow on the surface can be heard from far off. Allow your ears to tell you what the fish are doing.

By now, you should have some idea as to what is going on. Let's assume that the flat you are targeting has a fair amount of trees along the shoreline, along with a few grassy banks, which are clear and open. We'll also assume that it is mid-morning or midafternoon, during which time one side of the stream or the other should have some shade.

Stay low to avoid silhouetting yourself, and slowly move toward the tail of the flat. Then, from shore, make several casts and cover this area. Once you've done this, move upstream a few yards, and target the next section on the flat. If at all possible, fish from the bank. This will help you avoid spooking the fish. Whether you fish a remote stream that hardly receives any angling pressure or a popular one that receives plenty, your number-one job is to work it without alerting the fish to your presence.

But let's assume that the shoreline trees and brush along the next section of the flat are too thick to allow fishing from the bank. Now, you must enter the stream. By all means, enter the area you've just fished, and do it quietly. Stand at the edge, and keep your silhouette low and movements to a minimum. When it is necessary to move upstream, take only a few soft, well-placed steps. You can fairly well gauge the amount of commotion you make by watching the ripples emitted by your legs. Strive to keep these ripples to a minimum. Fish know that such ripples moving across the surface of an otherwise calm flat just isn't right, and they'll retreat to deeper or thicker cover.

In the event that the water in your stream is exceptionally clear (during the low-water conditions of summer, this is very often the case), you may consider kneeling on the stream bottom to reduce your silhouette. I realize that these techniques are reminiscent of those used on a tropical flat for bonefish or permit, but sometimes, this is exactly what you'll have to do in order to catch fish. Remember that bass holding on a shallow flat are usually nervous, and they'll flee at the slightest disturbance. On the other hand, if you do everything right, you'll occasionally pull out a fish that surpasses even your wildest expectations. Again, stealth is paramount.

Also, avoid kicking rocks, logs, and other objects. Sound travels five times faster in water than in air, and this is yet another way of alerting the fish to your presence. Such tactical sloppiness is a stream-fishing faux pas, and when it occurs you alert even those fish holding far from your immediate vicinity. Very often, you won't even see these fish because they will have all fled to deeper water or thick cover and away from you!

Another thing to consider is your own shadow. Don't ever allow your shadow to fall on water you intend to fish. Keep your silhouette as low as possible, and always consider the sun's position in the sky. This entails alternating your own position within a stream as the day progresses.

Take into consideration which side of the stream offers shade. If ample cover is available on both sides of the stream, not all of the fish will hold on the shaded side. But you can be sure that many of them, if not most, will. Shade also provides excellent cover for you, the angler. Make every attempt to approach and fish the stream from the shaded side. In the event that you plan to enter the stream, it is always advisable to fish the water where you plan to enter before getting in. You never know when your idea of perfect cover and a fish's will coincide.

Fish upstream, targeting any shade or other likely cover. Work the areas closest to you first, then gradually extend your casts until you've covered as much water as you possibly can before moving on. In some situations you can use the main current to conceal your movements, but this is seldom the case on a flat. This means that you'll have to fish across stream as well as upstream before moving on.

Let's assume that you've cast across the stream and taken a nice bass from an undercut bank or a laydown. Make another cast into the same area, and then another. Often, where you catch one fish, you'll catch another, for bass are gregarious creatures. Depending on the type of fly or lure you're using, you may wish to present a different offering before moving on to another area. This is a good idea.

In those instances when several fish are holding in the same area, usually the smaller ones are the first to strike. Perhaps this is because these fish know that because of their smaller size, they must jump at any feeding opportunity they can, lest another, larger fish get there first. Similarly, the larger fish are often less likely to take the first or even the second offering that they see. Large fish feed less frequently than smaller ones; they are wiser, more cautious. These fish must be finessed into biting.

If you're ever skeptical that larger fish are holding in the same area from which you've just hooked one fish, pay strict attention to your lure and the hooked fish as you fight and play it. Very often you'll see another—and much larger—fish following after its hooked mate. There are many theories as to why fish do this, but I believe that it's often a case of piscatorial jealousy. The larger fish weren't so easily fooled and, seeing its buddy darting about with what appears to be a meal hanging from its mouth, the larger bass becomes jealous. I've observed these "jealous" fish attempting to steal a lure or fly from the mouth of a hooked fish on many occasions. One such incident took place on a lake and involved quite a large smallmouth bass ramming its head into a striped bass twice its size. Visible from the striper's mouth was a good portion of the streamer fly it had just snatched up, and apparently the bronze fighter had its eyes locked onto this apparent meal as well. I couldn't help but notice that the hooked striper was receiving a considerable pummeling from the "jealous" smallie, if not the angler!

On another occasion, my father hooked a nice largemouth bass that looked like it would weigh 2 pounds or more. While fighting this fish, three shadows appeared right behind, tailing the hooked bass. The three shadows were largemouth bass ranging in size from about 2 pounds to more than 5. They began taking swipes at the hooked bass, oblivious to my father. They never got the lure from their mate's mouth, but several times during the spectacle, they rammed into my father's leg while trying to do so.

In any event, if a spot looks promising, don't ever fail to give it your complete attention to the tune of several different presentations. You just never know when there is a large fish lurking there, perhaps needing only a bit of finessing.

Some of the best lures for finessing fish are those that are designed to be worked slowly across the stream bottom. For conventional tackle, these include weedless jigs; soft plastics, such as worms, lizards, or tubes; and sometimes even spoons or suspending crankbaits. Another excellent choice is a soft-plastic bait-fish imitation or a soft jerkbait. Rig this lure without any weight, and allow it to slowly fall just beneath the surface, manipulating it with slight twitches and frequent pauses.

Fly-anglers often resort to crayfish patterns, bunny leeches, or even worm imitations. Woolly buggers are another good choice. The idea is to put the lure right in front of the fish and keep it there until it strikes. Sometimes, you may have to drop the fly into the target area, allow it to fall to the bottom, and just leave it there for as long as you can stand it. Then, the moment you finally move it is often when you'll get that strike. During winter, I catch probably half of my fish this way.

Regarding lure or fly choice, always take water clarity and temperature into consideration. In particularly stained or cloudy water, realize that your typical silver or chrome minnow offerings won't be nearly as effective. Instead, consider using colors such as gold, chartreuse, or red. Similarly, water temperature can tell you much about how the fish are behaving. To that end, it is always advisable to carry along a small-stream thermometer with which to make quick and accurate temperature readings. If the water in your stream is 70 degrees Fahrenheit or above, feel free to try rapid retrieves. If you're fishing during late fall or winter and the water temperature is hovering at 50 degrees or cooler, remember that a slow presentation is probably necessary for you to be successful. Of course, during winter the fish won't use the flats as heavily as they do during the warmer months, but there are always exceptions. As always, experiment until you find what the fish prefer, but use water temperature to put you in the ballpark.

Make the effort to present your offering into every inch of real estate within your target area before moving on. Make precise casts, and strive to keep the noise of your lure entering the water to a minimum. With casting tackle, this can often be accomplished by flipping or pitching, though because of your low angle when wading, this is often a tough proposition. This is where ultralight and fly tackle really shine, as they both excel in delicate presentations. When using the latter on a calm flat, long leaders are a definite asset.

Moving on, we come to a patch of weeds that extends from the bank well out into the water. Before making a cast, observe these weeds, and watch for any signs of abnormal movement. If you determine that the bass are holding within the weeds, you're going to have to get your bait into the thick stuff. Of course, weed-resistant lures are in order for such a situation, and they'll usually have to fall right in front of the fish to prompt a strike. This means that you'll have to make many casts, but you won't have to leave the fly or lure in any one spot for very long. The fish is either there, or it isn't. If the fish is there, most likely it will take your offering in an instant.

On the other hand, if you see no movement inside the weeds, get a minnow or frog imitation to the *outside* edge. If a bass is holding here, or even *just inside* the weeds, you can bet that it is waiting to take a swipe at precisely this sort of forage.

Some good flies for this sort of work include the Muddler Minnow, Clouser Floating Minnow, or any sort of shiner or sculpin pattern. Remember to work the sculpin fly close to the bottom. If these flies fail you, then try a woolly bugger or a crayfish pattern. If fish are present, these two standbys are seldom refused.

Once again, work the area nearest you first before extending your casts and presentations.

If any logs, rocks, or boulders are present on the flat, they deserve special attention. Minnow or other bait-fish patterns worked around this structure are seldom refused. One of the best lures is a shallow-running crankbait, which may be retrieved so that it bumps the structure on its way over or around the object. When this happens, look for the strike immediately thereafter, just as the lure presents itself on the opposite side.

Depressions or shallow holes are another good location to target. These areas frequently hold a fish or two, even on a flat, and should be explored with some sort of subsurface lure or fly. When they contain vegetation, you are almost guaranteed a strike. Crayfish, leech, and bait-fish imitations are some of the best offerings for bass holding in these features.

And thus, the remainder of the flat should be covered in this manner. Take care to move slowly, and thoroughly examine each and every bit of cover or structure before ruling it out. Working a flat this way helps prevent spooking fish, and it also affords you a greater opportunity at those larger, more reluctant fish. Sometimes, you'll be very surprised at the number and size of bass a shallow flat can hold, even during midday. More than once I've arrived at a stream, thinking of fishing several different areas, only to spend the majority of my time in one confined location, on a flat, catching fish as fast as I could present them with my offering. With practice, you'll be able to do the same.

128   GRAVEL BARS

Gravel bars may be found in many areas within a stream, including flats and pools, and in necked-down areas that often feature chutes, runs, and moderate to swift currents. They are often composed of pea gravel or small stones, and sometimes even sand or mud. Often, they are home to large numbers of minnows, shiners, and other baitfish. Occasionally, crayfish are even found in these areas. Gravel bars are excellent locations to target early and late in the day, but when they're located near a chute or run, they can hold fish anytime.

As with riffles and flats, gravel bars are usually best fished from the downstream side, retrieving your lure with the current. At times, it may be beneficial to fish this type of feature from across the stream, working the lure out into deeper water. During periods of low light, it is frequently possible to catch fish very near the bank in extremely shallow water. But the best area on a gravel bar is that on the opposite end, in deeper water. This is where the larger fish tend to hold.

When approaching a gravel bar (which should be done from the downstream side), make a series of fan casts to the near—or downstream—side, covering all water from the bank to the deeper side. As you might expect, bait-fish imitations are perfect for these areas. When gravel bars are found in relatively shallow and calm water, delicate presentations are in order to avoid spooking the fish, which tend to be quite skittish when holding here. You should also take care to use the lightest line possible. When water conditions are extremely clear, you may even find it helpful to go with fluorocarbon line. When the surface is broken and the current swift, this delicacy isn't normally required.

As the bar slopes off into the water, it tends to integrate into the stream bottom. Logs, rocks, and boulders are frequently found in these areas, just off the bar and situated in the deeper water. Sometimes, even chutes or small runs may be present on this deeper side of the stream. This is a prime area for bass, and it deserves special attention.

If I'm fishing a minnow imitation in such an area with little or no luck, I'll always switch to a bait that I can work along the bottom before moving on. Naturally, bottom baits can be fished more slowly and subtly than most minnow imitations and will often provoke strikes from reluctant bass. The more structure an area has, the more slowly and thoroughly it must be fished. So, switching to a jig or a bunny leech in this situation is a logical move. Regardless of the lure or fly you choose, ensure that you use one with a weed guard. There is no frustration quite like that derived from hanging up a lure in a prime area in which you've managed to get off only a cast or two. Incidentally, this is where toting two rods comes in handy. In the event you hang up, simply fit that rod into your waders, leaving the line as it is, and begin fishing with your other outfit. This affords you the opportunity to continue working the water without disturbing the area.

If the water is off-colored or stained, and I'm using conventional tackle, I'll frequently resort to a small, ⅛-ounce spinnerbait in chartreuse/white, yellow, orange, or red. The darker the water, the darker the lure. In some cases, I'll resort to a brown or even a black spinner, often one with gold or painted blades.

Spinnerbaits are tremendously effective. Part of the reason for this is that they may be retrieved in a variety of ways, and they may be fished in all depths of the water column. They are great burned just beneath the surface, so that they create a small wake; they may be "slow-rolled" along bottom; and they are great when retrieved in a vertical jigging fashion.

Once you've covered the deeper side of the gravel bar, move a few yards upstream so that you may fish the opposite side. Take care to use the bar to your advantage. Remain on the downstream side as you cast upstream; this will help conceal your approach. Once again, target the shallow water first, and gradually move out into the deeper side.

If you're fishing a stream in the middle of the day, you can be reasonably sure that few if any fish are to be found in the shallow water near the bank. Almost always, the deeper side is the place you'll want to target. Study the situation before making a cast, and when you've determined the location of any structure, proceed. Sometimes, a jerkbait worked just beneath the surface will draw a few strikes; other times, you'll need to work a little deeper into the water column. Working your lure over any visible logs or rocks is always advisable, and if you can make your offering come into contact with this structure, you're almost guaranteed a strike if any fish are present. To that end, shallow-running crankbaits are excellent medicine for fish holding in these areas. Retrieve your lure so that it bumps a log or rock, and be ready.

Plastic tubes are another excellent bait for working the deep end of a bar, as they can be manipulated to imitate many different forage items, including baitfish, leeches, or crayfish. They can be used with a swimming retrieve, jigged, or worked along bottom. For most situations, I like a small, 2- to 3-inch tube. Some of my most productive colors are white, black, pumpkinseed, and watermelon. I'll typically rig these baits Texas-style with a 1/0 or 2/0 off-shanked hook, though they're also effective with a Carolina drop-shot rig or a weedless jig head so designed for the size of tube you're fishing. Tubes are another incredibly versatile bait that you should have in your small-stream arsenal.

One lure that has worked particularly well for me along

the deep end of gravel bars is a simple concoction that is seldom used anymore. I take a size-4 hook with a wire weed guard and attach a small, white pork trailer. That's it. I fish this lure with the current and allow it to bump and flutter over any bottom structure. This offering mimics an injured baitfish, and the pork scent further tantalizes the bass. And once a bass commits, the realistic flavor and texture urge the fish to hold onto the lure, allowing me more time to set the hook.

In the fly department, I like Zonker patterns for the deep side of gravel bars. Two of my best colors are white and olive, and black is an excellent choice for night. Like plastic tubes, Zonkers can be retrieved in a variety of ways, including swimming them horizontally or crawling them along the bottom. One of my favorite ways to work a Zonker is to fit a small split shot about 10 inches up the leader from the fly. Then, using a lift-and-drop technique with my fly-rod, I use something of a vertical retrieve with the fly. This is much like fishing with a plastic worm, and it is exceptionally productive in post—cold-front conditions.

Almost any lure or fly can be made to work when fishing gravel bars, though frequently you'll have to get it down deep and contact the bottom structure. Once again, this often entails the use of a weedless bait, which should be worked slowly for best results.

CHUTES AND RUNS

Whenever I encounter a chute or run, regardless of size, my heart gets to thumping. These areas almost always hold bass, at any time of day. They're often characterized by their slightly deeper water and sometimes a faster current. What makes them so productive is that they serve as something of a highway for the bass, allowing them to move freely about a stream while still affording a certain degree of cover and safety. Some of the best chutes and runs occur just below a waterfall or riffles, connecting such areas to pools or flats.

I prefer to fish chutes and runs with a fly-rod, and my favorite fly for this sort of a situation is a white Deceiver, which is only lightly weighted, in sizes ranging from 6 to 1. In stained water, however, I'll often resort to chartreuse or orange. Black bass, especially the smallmouth, love these two colors.

These features are also excellent locations to use nymph patterns, especially when fish are holding tight to the bottom. Some of the best are stonefly nymphs in sizes 8 to 12, tumbled along the bottom. A highly visible strike indicator, and sometimes two, may be required in certain conditions.

Although chutes and runs themselves are deeper than the surrounding water, I would still classify them as shallow. In most of the streams that I fish, they tend to run from 2 to 4 feet, sometimes deeper and other times shallower. With this in mind, I always use a floating line and long leaders, usually something in the 9- to 10-foot range. When the water over a chute is fairly swift, you can often get away with using a shorter leader, but I seldom go less than 6 feet for these situations.

Because they hold deeper and often faster water, you may think that you can move in very close to fish holding in a chute or run. This is seldom the case, for these features are usually surrounded by shallow water, and the fish here are very sight oriented. They are accustomed to watching the shallows for their prey; consequently, they will easily spot you in the event you try to walk up on them. This makes long casts mandatory. Obviously, chutes and runs are best fished from downstream and to one side.

Whenever I encounter one of these features, I always fish

the tail end first, thoroughly covering the area with short casts. Then, I reach out and deliver the fly as far as possible, making every effort to reach the head or beginning of the feature. Of course, they're fished by working your fly downstream with the current, along the duration of the feature. The main reason that I refrain from moving in to work farther upstream is that the bass frequently swim back and forth, from the chute's head to tail, like aquatic sentries. Thus, they would easily spot me.

On a positive note, however, just because you don't connect with a fish at the chute's tail doesn't mean that you won't do so fifteen minutes later. As I said earlier, chutes and runs are like highways, and as is the case with these main thoroughfares, traffic is always moving.

Keeping a low silhouette is important here, as is the use of drab or camouflage clothing. If one fish sights you, you can be sure that it is going to scatter; in doing so it will probably alert all of the fish in the area. This makes sidearm casts preferable to long, overhand casts. Sometimes, all it takes is the flash of your line or leader flying through the air to alert the fish. A sidearm cast, with your line low and parallel to the surface, helps prevent this.

If I'm fishing a miniature chute or run, one with especially calm water, I'll use a lightweight fly-rod, such as a 4- or 5-weight. And yes, I often carry more than one rod with me when I fish a small stream. I have been known to carry as many as three rods, sticking those not in use into my waders until the situation calls for them.

At any rate, lighter-weight lines make much less commotion when they fall onto the surface. When using light rods and lines, you'll also want to scale down your offering. You can increase the strength and size of your leader only so much; ultimately, it is the fly line that is going to get the job done.

134 Whatever you do, strive to imitate with your fly the size and shape of your stream's natural baitfish. But allow the water conditions to influence your choice of color.

When fishing these features with conventional tackle, I'll almost always use a light-action spinning rod with either a ⅛-ounce floating jerkbait or a spinnerbait of similar size. Work your lure all over the area, covering the chute or run itself, as well as the ledges on either side. It is also advisable to work the stream bank nearest to the chute, as fish will often hold here while awaiting the current to bring them food. If you ever encounter a situation in which the chute or run is located near a bank that offers overhanging brush or any aquatic vegetation, then slow down and work the area over with every lure in your tackle box if necessary. When this sort of situation exists in a small stream, you can bet that it will hold fish, and probably a large one.

Chapter 8

Fishing Deep Water

I N A SMALL STREAM, "deep" water may range from 3 to 6 feet. Although some streams contain much deeper water, these are—more often than not—the exception. As I mentioned earlier, the word "deep" is relative. Your stream may have numerous pools and holes that plunge to 7 or 8 feet. Other streams, conversely, may hold only 3 or 4 feet of water at their deepest point. Our discussion of fishing deep water, then, will concentrate on the deepest areas of your stream, which are most often the pools or holes.

I used to believe that pools were always best fished from downstream, at any time and any place. I no longer feel this way. It has been my experience that many pools are simply too long or too deep to fish exclusively from the downstream side. Also, there is the factor of reverse currents(eddies and such), in which the fish tend to face into the current in the direction *opposite* from the main flow.

Some pools are inundated with such a great deal of

shoreline cover that the only way to effectively fish them is by moving in from upstream. Similarly, some of the Ozark streams I've fished, as well as some of those in east Texas, have pools that are much too deep and long to work only from the downstream side. Many of these pools also possess heavy shoreline cover and thus disallow any bank or across-stream fishing. Therefore, the only way to effectively target the entire pool is to fish part of it from upstream.

The reason that I no longer believe that fishing a pool from the downstream side is the single best method is that I've caught too many fish, both large and small specimens, by working them from all directions. The bottom line for fishing pools is that you have to present your fly or lure into every nook and cranny, and to accomplish this, you must exercise all options. If this entails fishing half of the pool from upstream, so be it. Or, if you have to walk the banks in order to shoot a lure into the thick cover across the stream, then by all means, get after it. You can't catch fish if you can't present them with your offering.

Of course, much of this adversity can be avoided by using some sort of small watercraft. This is an excellent way to reach remote or inhospitable areas of a stream, and if you're given to portaging, paddling, and the like, then by all means have at it. I, however, enjoy walking the banks and wading. I've also found very few pools that I have been unable to fish from one angle or the other. In fact, I relish stalking the banks, looking for places to make a quick cast or two. My focus is on presenting the fish with my lure without them knowing of my presence. I feel as though I can best accomplish this by walking or wading and leaving the boat, canoe, or float tube at home. But you'll need to make your own call on this.

When you come to a pool you wish to fish, you should have first scouted the area and learned of its unique, indi-

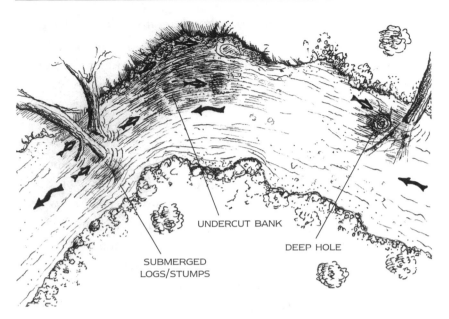

UNDERCUT BANK

DEEP HOLE

SUBMERGED
LOGS/STUMPS

Deep water always holds fish. When it contains additional
cover like logs, stumps, or an undercut bank, it is likely to
harbor the largest fish in the stream.

vidual characteristics. This, of course, would tell you what the
pool's major structural features are and where they're located.
You would have also noticed how deep it is, what kind of
shoreline cover is present, and the bottom composition, as
well as several other important features.

Are there any well-worn trails leading to the pool? Any
bare spots along the bank, which may have been worn smooth
by dozens of pairs of feet standing on them? If so, avoid these
areas. This is not to say that you can't catch fish from them,
only that you're less likely to. You have to remember that
these fish are accustomed to seeing both anglers and their lures
from these predictable locations. You need to try something
that the fish aren't used to seeing. If you're intent on fishing
these common areas, then please do so, but don't overlook the

138   advantages of approaching the matter from a different and un-
common angle.

If it were me, I'd simply look for another pool. But, in the
absence of another, I'd position myself in the pool's most difficult and inhospitable reaches, where other anglers aren't
likely to have trodden before. In many cases, *this* is where
you'll catch the best fish in a pool.

So, we have a major interstate, which is the current, running through the middle of our pool. At the pool's head,
below the riffles or falls, the current is strong and reasonably
fast. As it enters the pool, it slows and gradually gains in
strength as it approaches the tail. The head and tail, then, are
like merging and exiting ramps on the interstate, as they concentrate traffic. Similarly, you can be sure that the fish will be
concentrated in such areas.

But then there is the pool's primary structural feature,
such as that large boulder, log, deadfall, or pile of rocks, perhaps 5 or 6 feet below the surface. This is the truck stop along
the interstate. Have you ever seen a truck stop that wasn't
busy? One without several oversized rigs idle and resting, refueling, or simply loitering about? I haven't either. And when
you find the pool's main structural feature, you can bet that
there are several fish in its vicinity, probably the largest fish,
and that they're either resting, refueling, or maybe even loitering about, waiting to pick on some unsuspecting minnow
or crayfish. Once in a while, you'll even encounter one of
these brutes that thinks it can leave the truck stop, rush out
onto the interstate, and cut off your lure without so much as
a courtesy signal. These violent collisions, you'll soon discover, frequently result in broken line, destroyed lures, bent
hooks, and medleys of wide eyes, head scratches, and four-
letter words.

It can be difficult and time-consuming to do, but it is

highly important to spend some time scouting the particular pool you intend to fish. The better the pool looks, the more time you should spend investigating. But this time isn't all lost; the more time you spend learning about a pool's features, the more productive fishing time you'll enjoy later.

I once spent a few days fishing a Tennessee stream, which I understood to be outstanding in the smallmouth and spotted (Kentucky) bass departments. On the first day of fishing, I found an exceptionally large, deep pool that may as well have had a neon sign above it flashing BASS HERE. It was such an inviting pool that I couldn't wait to get my line in the water. After fishing this water for four hours, I had seven fish to show for my efforts. Not bad, but I knew that I could do better. I spent the remainder of the afternoon scouting the pool.

I must have covered the pool from every angle, from every possible direction, from both banks, and from upstream, downstream, across stream and in-between stream. I was all over the pool, looking, listening, and searching. Fishing would have been more fun, but I would have failed to notice the pool's underlying characteristic had I not taken the time to scour the place.

Situated perhaps halfway through the pool and centered in what looked to be its deepest water was a smaller pool, with steep ledges and large rocks within. It was a pool within the pool. And this pool within the pool, I noticed, looked to be roughly 2 feet deeper than the surrounding bottom, which I estimated at 5 or so feet. So with 7 feet of water and rocks and ledges to break the current and provide ambushing stations, can you take a guess as to where the fish were?

With a bird's-eye view, I spent forty minutes or so examining just that small pool within the larger pool. The water was reasonably clear and I could make out the dark, rounded shapes of the rocks and some other grayish, oblong objects.

These objects didn't move much, and it was only through keen observation of the area that I was able to determine that these oblong shapes were fish. Occasionally, the shadows would move or I'd see a bright flash in the water as one would move up to nab a meal and then turn on its side on its way back into the small pool. From where I had been standing when fishing the lower end of the pool, I was just missing the tail end of this smaller, deeper pool. So, I looked for a way to reach it without alerting the fish. With my game plan set, I returned to the stream bright and early the next morning.

Thereupon, I proceeded to catch 12 fish over the course of the first hour, including 2 that measured more than 16 inches. When I released these wild smallmouth back into the water, I didn't fail to notice where they went: right back into the smaller, deeper pool from whence they came.

If only you'll spend some time scouting, it will all seem so easy and clear. Your resulting epiphany will reveal those areas where the fish are most likely to hold. And you will see the light.

Once you've scouted and determined the best place within the pool, you can then decide how to fish it. This is why we don't just blunder into a pool and begin fishing. Maybe the best area is on the opposite end, near the head, or perhaps it's located in the middle. Always consider your options.

How deep is the water? Is it too deep to wade in from downstream? If so, consider the banks. How thick is the shoreline cover? Does it permit you to move in close enough to present a lure? Or do the banks rise high above the water, or feature thick and impenetrable brush? If this is out, move upstream. Where, exactly, can you enter the stream? Will the fish see you when you enter? If so, how can you avoid this?

This is the toughest aspect of fishing a pool. Deciding where to position yourself so as to avoid alerting the fish, while finding a place that simultaneously affords you the opportunity to effectively present your fly or lure into the target area is probably the single most important variable in this pool-fishing equation. If one variable is out of whack, the entire equation fails. This is why you must examine every angle, every possible approach to get to the fish, whether this means coming in from upstream, downstream, or from the bank.

Downstream is theoretically a good angle because you approach the fish from behind. But what about the fish holding along either bank in the reverse current? Because we're fishing in small creeks and streams, they're liable to see you, as they're not far away.

The way we deal with this is to first scout the situation from the bank. If there are fish holding near the pool's tail or along either bank in this area, then the tail must be fished before moving into the area. Furthermore, you'll have to fish it from far enough downstream so that the fish don't see you. Take advantage of any cover or special contours the stream offers in order to conceal yourself. Once you work this area *thoroughly*, you can then move into the tail of the pool and fish upstream.

What about moving into a pool from upstream? Sometimes, this is your only option, but it presents some difficulties. One is that the debris you kick up will wash downstream and possibly alert the fish. This is bad, so don't do it. When at all possible, stay to one side of the stream, next to the bank, and make your casts from here.

Another potential problem is that the trees and brush along the shoreline might inhibit your casting. You can learn some new casts, which is always advisable, or you can leave the area and look for another way in. The former is preferable, as it will increase your confidence, which in itself will increase your catch *exponentially*.

Yet another dilemma with approaching a pool from the upstream side is the issue of the fish spotting you. This is to be avoided if you are to have any hope of connecting with your quarry. You can help alleviate this problem by remaining far back from the stream edge, keeping a low profile, and using any available cover to your advantage. This limits your casting range, I know, but this is where a fly-rod shines.

Tie on a large, gaudy stonefly nymph and, standing well off the bank where the fish can't see you, cast out into the stream. Longer rods, in the 9-foot range, will make this job easier. You should strive to drift your nymph downstream, through the target area. A strike indicator helps, and sometimes it may take two or three to do the job properly. Polarizing glasses are instrumental for keeping tabs on your line and indicators. When you get a strike, move close enough to the stream so that you can fight and land the fish without injuring it.

For those trout anglers who have fished spring creeks, this technique is nothing new. Follow the same procedures when the situation so demands, and you'll easily find success on the bass stream.

Cover this section of the pool before moving in close and creeping downstream, keeping your silhouette low as you work from either bank. At this point, you can fish the pool in whatever fashion you wish, but remember the fly-rod when you have trouble getting a lure into a tight spot. These tools are without equal insofar as delivering a fly upstream and allowing it to drift down into the red zone is concerned. In this sort of a situation, conventional lures would likely snag or spook the fish upon crashing in right over their heads.

Once you've covered all you can by working from the pool's upstream side, or if you're simply opposed to moving in from this direction, then you always have the banks from which to fish.

Like the other areas, banks also present special advantages
and drawbacks. Probably their greatest benefit is that you
don't have to enter the water to fish, and the very glaring advantage of this is that you tend to spook fewer fish.

On the other hand, some banks are steep and high,
whereas others are so densely covered in brush, briars, trees,
and vines that you couldn't possibly fish from them. And
those that are relatively open, permitting easy casting, are frequently too steep and tall to safely land a fish. Your only re-
course in such situations is to simply root around until you
find something more suitable. Short of this, you always have
the other bank. But if both banks prove to be impenetrable
barriers to a pool's flanks, then it's back into the stream, where
you'll have to make long casts in order to cover as much water
as possible.

Conversely, in the event that you are able to fish from the
bank, you'll almost always do better by using any existing
shade or other cover to your advantage. After all, this is how
the fish hide from you, and consider how difficult they are to
detect. When you do find a suitable spot from which to cast,
it is highly advisable to stay put for a while and keep your
movements to a minimum. Fish instinctively respond to any
movement along the banks because they know that these
areas harbor predators. I've often had my best luck fishing
pools after I positioned myself in an area for thirty minutes or
more, with my only movements being those involved with
casting.

Now that you have an idea about how to approach pools, let's
talk about how to fish them.

Pools lend themselves to a variety of offerings, from surface flies to shallow- and midrunning plugs to bottom baits.
This is because of their deeper water, and on any given day,

the fish may be more active in one level of the water column than the other. Let's begin with surface lures.

SURFACE LURES AND FLIES

Traditionally, surface lures were used primarily during mornings and evenings. This is due to many factors, including the lower light angle and the fact that bass are often more active during this time, when their eyesight is superior to that of the baitfish. Surface plugs encompass all of those that are designed to float and be manipulated on top of the water. These include poppers, chuggers, sputterers, buzzbaits, torpedoes, and even such baits as floating worms and insect patterns. These lures are indeed effective early and late in the day, but they may also produce well during the middle of the day, when the sun is high and bright.

The key to working surface baits is to draw the fish's attention to them. This is why so many of these offerings are noisemakers; the fish have to realize that a potential meal is present if they are to rush up from the bottom and grab it. Thus, these baits often appeal to a fish's sense of sight, sound, or vibration, which bass detect with their lateral lines. Those that lack noisemaking devices, such as insect and worm patterns, are primarily sight baits, which are usually more effective in shallow water and in those areas offering plenty of weed growth and other vegetation.

Naturally, it stands to reason that you'll often have your best luck with, say, a floating dragonfly pattern by using it early or late in the day and working it near weed beds, cattails, and lily pads, where bass are likely to be found. These baits don't emit much sound; it is primarily the sight of such a lure fluttering or floating on the surface that attracts the bass.

You can also have tremendous success with surface lures

Stealth is the order of the day on the small bass stream. Wearing camouflage or drab clothing and using any shoreline cover to mask your silhouette will help you catch more fish.

during the middle of the day. The key here is to concentrate on the shaded side of the stream and work your lure as far back into the cover as you dare. Sometimes, you'll have your best luck by pitching a popper just into the inside edge of the shade, whereas other times you must get your lure far back into this cover to catch bass. In this case, presenting your fly right up next to the bank is often the ticket to success.

Skating dry flies is yet another effective technique, especially in pools and around their weed edges. Although mornings and evenings are the most productive times for skating flies, this technique draws fish to the surface at all hours of the day. Under an overcast sky, it can be extremely effective.

Skating is best performed with large flies, and Wulff, Coachman, and Irresistible patterns are all excellent producers in sizes 8 through 12.

Water temperature plays a key role in the effectiveness of surface lures. During winter, when water temperatures are often well below 50 degrees Fahrenheit, the bass's metabolism is greatly reduced, and the fish, needing only a fraction of the food that they do in the warmer months, are lethargic and extremely reluctant to move very far to grab a meal. In this situation, a surface plug is not likely to be effective.

During the warmer months, however, from spring to early fall, when water temperatures range from about 60 to 80 degrees or so, surface lures can be deadly. Actually, 70- to 80-degree water temperatures are generally best for this sort of work. During these times, bass are much more active and aggressive, and a fish's strike zone increases proportionately.

In my experience, the only viable exception to these rules involves the smallmouth bass. The bronze fighter, being the highly pugnacious creature that it is, sometimes forgets that it is winter and 45 degrees and occasionally rushes to the surface to pummel a lure. This isn't too terribly common, but it does happen in all waters where smallies are found.

SUBSURFACE LURES AND FLIES

We can classify subsurface lures into two general categories: those designed to fish at middepths and the bottom lures. We'll first discuss the former—those lures designed to work just beneath the surface and down to several feet in the middepths. This category can include almost all manner of baits, from streamers and nymphs to crankbaits, jerkbaits, tubes, jigs, spinners, and many others. Some baits, such as plastic tubes and jigs, are actually designed for bottom work, but may be used very effectively in the middepths.

Midrunning lures usually target those fish that are either actively feeding, suspended, or sometimes even holding on bottom. They may be used with fly, spinning, or casting tackle and are effective with a variety of different retrieves. During the warmer months, midrunning lures probably account for the majority of the fish I catch in small streams.

Of course, the idea here is to mimic the natural forage on which the bass are feeding. As with everything else, this is accomplished through careful scouting. Once the specific type of forage is identified, strive to imitate it with your lure or fly.

Water clarity plays an important role when fishing midrunning lures. When fishing clear water, especially on bright days, I tend to use white or chartreuse/white streamer patterns. Or, if I'm fishing with spinning or casting tackle, I'll lean toward silver, chrome, or pearl lures, regardless of shape or size.

When the water is stained or cloudy, I go with darker colors, such as gold, orange, red, brown, or even black in some cases.

There is a great debate today as to whether the addition of eyes increases a lure's or fly's effectiveness. Some maintain that eyes are vital to a good lure or fly and help trigger strikes; others disagree. In my experience, eyes are unimportant to a surface lure, on which the bass probably wouldn't be able to see them anyway, but they are absolutely essential to a subsurface lure. I'm not alone in this contention, for many of today's best subsurface lures feature incredibly convincing and lifelike 3D or holographic eyes. I'm not saying that subsurface lures that lack eyes won't catch fish; I'm simply suggesting that those that have them are better lures, and they will catch more fish. After all, it has been scientifically documented that bass and many other predator species focus on their prey's eyes just before attacking.

Rattles are another feature of many of today's midrunning

lures. These noisemakers generally feature some sort of internal chamber that contains a few steel pellets. When retrieved, these lures clack and rattle, which helps provoke fish into striking. Personally, I like such lures and use them whenever I can. I often have my best luck with them when fishing in stained or cloudy water, when visibility is reduced.

When fishing a midrunning lure or fly in a pool, always begin by fishing higher in the water column, and gradually work deeper and deeper. This way, you first target those fish that are positioned nearer the surface, more active, and more willing to come up and take your offering. Then, by working deeper, you have a chance at those fish that are suspending or holding on bottom and reluctant to come up for a meal. Another advantage is that you stand less of a chance of spooking the fish in a given area by first taking those positioned higher in the water column. Obviously, if you hook a fish holding on bottom and the fish fights and struggles its way higher into the water column, his buddies are likely to spook.

When fishing a midrunning lure, don't just cast into the middle of the pool and begin cranking. This can work (surprisingly well at times), but you'll be far more successful if you target isolated bits of cover, such as weed beds, laydowns, rock piles, and the like. These areas are likely ambushing positions for bass.

At times, you can rig some unusual arrangements, which will help you catch reluctant fish. One that I frequently use with casting or spinning tackle involves a lure and a dropper rig, much like those used when fly-fishing for trout. The lure that I most often go with is a small, ⅛-ounce jig, to which I attach a plastic curly-tailed grub. I'll attach this lure to my line using a Palomar knot. Then, using an improved clinch knot, I'll attach a 16-inch leader to the hook of this lure. I then use a larger lure, such as a jerkbait, preferably a suspending model, for the dropper. Sometimes, I'll even go with a lightweight crankbait if I determine that the lure's action would be beneficial in a given situation. If the outfit runs a little deeper than you'd like, either lighten your lures or attach a small cork or float to your leader in order to make the outfit more buoyant.

Throw this rig out into the pool, and begin a slow retrieve. When connected and retrieved properly, it roughly mimics a larger fish pursuing a smaller one. This is often all it takes to provoke a jarring strike from any nearby bass, and it works especially well on larger specimens.

Finally, we can't forget soft-plastic jerkbaits. These baits are designed to imitate baitfish, such as shad and minnows, and do so surprisingly well. They work well both with and without the addition of weights, but when I use these lures I usually omit the weight so that the lure runs just beneath the surface. Like hard-plastic jerkbaits, these soft models are sight baits. Many incorporate some sort of shiny or flashy finish, whereas others feature a reflective prism inside their transparent bodies.

The idea is to cast the lure and allow it to sink just beneath the surface, no more than a foot or so. Then, use sharp twitches to give the lure action. This mimics a struggling baitfish so well that bass will often rush up from the bottom of a pool to strike.

One other capability of these lures is that they may be rigged completely weedless, just like a worm or lizard. This allows you to fish them in tight, brushy areas where large fish are likely to hold.

Whatever you do, don't forget to add a few different sizes and colors of these baits into your tackle box. They work all year long, but are especially effective in the early spring, late summer, and fall.

Fly-fishers can also approach reluctant bass by using an intermediate line and bait-fish imitation. The fly should have a good deal of flash material built in so as to further attract the bass. Cast out and begin an erratic retrieve, with intermittent pauses. Experiment with retrieval speed and cadence until you find what works best, and in really cold weather don't be afraid to simply pause and allow the lure to slowly descend the bottom.

BOTTOM LURES AND FLIES

Bottom lures are my favorite when fishing during winter, after cold fronts, and when targeting finicky bass. These lures consist of jigs; soft-plastic tubes, worms, lizards, grubs, centipedes, crayfish, and other molds; and even some spinnerbaits and crankbaits. There are also some great bottom lures available to the fly-angler in the form of nymphs, crayfish, sculpin, and other bait-fish patterns. These flies work well not only on the bottom, but anywhere near it. And they work all year long.

Sometimes, bottom offerings are the only ones I'll use when fishing a stream, especially if I know that the fish are sluggish or holding deep because of the current weather and water conditions. During summer, when the air temperature is 90 or 100 degrees Fahrenheit and the water 80 or so—during which time the fish gravitate to deeper, well-oxygenated areas, such as those below waterfalls or riffles—I'll frequently use a plastic tube or crayfish fly. Similarly, in winter, when you may fish all day and only get three or four bites, I tend to lean toward sculpin-imitating flies, weedless jigs, and small grubs, working them slowly across bottom.

Generally, bottom lures lend themselves best to a slow presentation. Usually, the slower the better. Slow presentations are ideal when the bass are finicky or reluctant to

When fishing pools, work all depths of the water column. Often, bass that are reluctant to come up and hit a surface lure will take one worked across the bottom.

commit, as they give the fish an extended opportunity to observe your offering and—if it's a convincing one—further enticement to strike. Furthermore, lethargic fish are extremely reluctant to move very far to chase down a lure. A slow-moving presentation, especially one interspersed with considerable pauses, keeps your lure in the magic window for as long as possible.

As always, strive to match your lure or fly to the natural you are imitating. The flip side to this is that the fish have to be able to find your offering; if the light is low or the water murky, then darker colors tend to produce better than lighter ones, even though the latter may more closely resemble the

152   natural forage. Just remember to imitate the natural's size and shape with your fly, and allow the water and light conditions to influence your choice of color.

While a bass's sight may be the best sense to exploit with your bottom lure, it's also important that your offering appeal to its sense of smell, sound, and even taste. When fishing with bottom lures, these senses are best exploited with conventional tackle. Flies tend to appeal primarily to a fish's sight, unless of course, you're given to spraying your offering with a scent attractant. Also, conventional lures are usually heavier and are often outfitted with rattles, glass beads, and such, which the fish can hear. They are commonly salt- or garlic-impregnated, which the fish can smell and taste, once they strike. Although the use of flies for bottom work can be very effective, when the water drops below about 45 degrees Fahrenheit, you'll have better luck with conventional lures. Of course, you probably have your own favorite methods and equipment, so by all means, use that which gives you confidence.

One important note on bottom lures is that they don't have to be used exclusively on the stream bottom to catch fish. Sometimes, they work exceptionally well as they're descending to the bottom. Tubes and jigs are a good example.

Plastic tubes are erratic baits. Each time a tube descends toward the bottom, it falls in a different trajectory than the last. Thus, when you jig or manipulate a tube in the water, it is constantly doing something different and erratic. This is, essentially, like making several different presentations with one cast. Sometimes these lures spiral, tumble, flip, or just shoot straight down. Because of this, they drive bass wild, triggering strikes even from reluctant fish. These erratic characteristics make tubes highly effective in deeper areas with abundant plant or weed growth, where bass are likely to hold and intercept the bait on its way down. Of course, you can modify the lure's rate of descent by alternating its weight. For a very slow fall, try rigging the hook weedless and omitting the weight. You can also slip a piece of foam or cork into the tube's hollow body for added buoyancy.

Jigs, too, are another bottom bait that can really catch a lot of fish when presented vertically. Weedless jigs range in size from tiny, $\frac{1}{16}$-ounce models to massive 1-ounce sizes and up. These lures come with a variety of different head shapes, each designed to give that particular jig a specific attribute. Some stand on end, some are better for working over smooth bottoms, and others excel in traversing gravel or rocky substrates. At any rate, they are all designed to be worked across the bottom.

But like the plastic tube, jigs often trigger reaction bites as they descend. It is difficult to say for just what a bass mistakes a vertically moving jig, but they obviously perceive it as some sort of forage item that is "here today, gone tomorrow." In this situation, a bass's instincts take over. These fish are programmed to strike at fleeing forage and will often hit descending jigs simply because they appear to be escaping, and this triggers their predatory nature.

You can manipulate this instinct by dropping a jig into a likely area, maintaining contact with your descending lure, and hoping that a bass takes it on the fall. This will happen more often than you might think. Because of your low angle when wading, pitching or flipping your bait can be difficult or even impossible at times. But this is exactly the type of cast you need to make, for it is highly important to drop the jig into the water with as little noise as possible. Inasmuch as we're dropping these baits practically right on the bass's head, a loud entry would surely scare the fish.

When you intend to fish a pool this way, it is better to get

Never overlook a good waterfall, for they very often hold large bass.

out of the water and work from either the edge of the stream or even the bank. Here you have a higher angle from which to work and are better able to flip or pitch your lure where it will land with a light *plop*.

But you can further tantalize the fish into striking by modifying your jig with some sort of trailer, whether pork or plastic.

A trailer can do many things for you. It can add to the bait's overall profile, turning a small jig into a substantial meal; it can appeal to the fish's sense of smell, as many pork and garlic-impregnated plastics do; and it can cause a bass to hold onto the lure longer, once it has committed to striking, as a result of its realistic flavor and texture. But perhaps even more importantly (especially because we're discussing vertical presentations), a trailer can slow the fall of your lure, thus increasing its time in the strike zone. This attribute is terribly important when flipping or pitching into cover, for often that extra second or two that the lure remains in front of the fish is what it takes to connect. If we could increase the time all of our lures and flies spend in the proverbial strike zone by even a second or two, we would substantially improve our success ratio.

Small trailers are fine for shallow or moderately deep water and are often the perfect accompaniment to a small jig. But for deep water and especially finicky fish, I like to use a small jig with a *large* pork trailer. This large trailer acts as something of a parachute on the small, lightweight jig and really reduces its rate of descent, which further tantalizes the fish.

Sometimes, jigs are best used by moving them across the stream bottom. This can entail hopping the jig along bottom, dragging it horizontally, or even ripping it up high and allowing it to fall. When I want to cover a lot of water, I typically use the last presentation. At such times, I'll frequently use a pork leech trailer and split the strip in half with my pocketknife. This gives the lure a bit of added action.

During winter, on the other hand, I find that moving a jig slowly across the bottom is the best approach. I begin by casting out and allowing the jig to settle on the bottom, then slowly hopping or draging it back towards me. The key to fishing a jig during winter is to keep it on or near the bottom and frequently pause the lure. I find that pausing for fifteen or twenty seconds, and sometimes a minute or more, is usually the key to getting bitten during winter. Though you aren't imparting any movement to the jig, it does exhibit some movement while at rest. The current causes the skirt and trailer to flutter and undulate ever so slightly, which arouses the fish's

156 curiosity. Often, a bass will move in close and examine the lure for a half-minute or more before committing. In fact, this is typical of winter bass. If you can encourage a bass to move in and examine your lure, you have a good chance of catching that fish. Keeping the jig on bottom and pausing are the crucial factors of success.

During the warmer months, when fish seek relief from the heat by holding on or near the bottom, I like to cast a jig, allow it to settle on the bottom and then begin a slow, steady retrieve. On this sort of retrieve, the jig remains in contact with the stream bottom, bumping over rocks, logs, and any other object along the way. This is very similar to fishing a jig during winter, only you don't have to go quite so slowly. For this presentation, I like a single-tail grub as a trailer, as the tail's added movement attracts the attention of any nearby bass. If a slow, steady retrieve doesn't work for you, try pausing the lure for ten seconds or so.

I mentioned earlier that spinnerbaits are also frequently used as bottom baits. They are especially effective when worked over or near grass beds, which tend to hold bass. For this sort of work, willow-leaf blades are ideal. They provide maximum snag resistance as your lure works through the cover.

Another good time to use spinners is when the pool you're fishing contains a good deal of logs and other woody structure. Dragging a spinnerbait over the logs, then allowing it to fall once it reaches the other side, can be deadly when the action has turned off on a hot summer day.

When a pool's substrate is composed of rock, sand, or gravel and is relatively open, I like working crankbaits across the bottom. The key here is using a lure that will dive to the necessary depth. Obviously, working a shallow-running model in a pool that holds 6 feet of water won't produce the desired

effect. You have to get the lure to the bottom and allow it to   *157*
do its work.

　　With this technique, I usually attempt to imitate a fleeing
crayfish with my lure. Hence, I'll use something red, brown, or
orange in color, and I'll retrieve it quickly across the bottom.
For this, you'll need a sensitive rod in order to discriminate between the thump of the bait as it bounces over the bottom and
the actual strike. With many models of crankbaits, you can
easily free a snagged lure simply by pausing and allowing it to
float up and away from the offending obstruction. Then,
simply continue your retrieve, but be ready for a vicious strike,
as they often come immediately thereafter.

Chapter 9

Night Fishing

FISHING AT NIGHT has a charm all its own. On a bass stream, there are no crowds after dark; even the most elusive of fish become active, and solitude takes on an entirely new meaning. Trophy trout hunters who seek the largest brown trout often go out at night, when these fish are most active. Sometimes, the streams that harbor such brutes can become quite crowded as word gets around that people are catching fish. But bass streams, especially small ones, are usually overlooked, ignored, or forgotten. While this holds true for days, it also applies—exponentially so—to nights.

There are many reasons why few anglers fish at night. It is often inconvenient. Perhaps it throws a kink into your schedule, or maybe you'll miss some sleep if you go. Some anglers are even scared to be out on a stream at night. But as a trophy bass guide who specializes in taking his clients out after dark once told me, "One must be dedicated to one's art."

On the other hand, there are many, many reasons to use a nocturnal routine, but two of the most important are that it affords you time on the water during which the fish are highly active and, during the warmer months, it allows you to beat the heat. The latter reason bears a high correlation to the former, for during summer many bass become almost entirely nocturnal in their habits. If you live in the South, where the summers are long and hot, nights provide you with the maximum fishing time under optimal conditions. And the hotter and more miserable the days, the better the fishing will be at night.

Conversely, if you're limited to days, you'll find that your most productive time on the water is limited to maybe a couple of hours after dawn and an hour or so before dusk. For me, this is simply unacceptable. When I want to fish, I want to fish, and I don't want to be bothered with time or weather constraints. I simply work with them and use them to my advantage.

The bottom line is that if you wish to fish, you have to make the time to go. And seldom is there any better time than after dark.

If you've ever fished for black bass in a small stream at night, if you've ever waded waist-deep into a pool and felt the wash from a fish jetting past your leg, the shoreline chorus of frogs and insects in full swing, and nature's sentries—owls and coyotes—announcing that all is well, then you know what I'm talking about. But if you're not accustomed to this sort of an adventure, then you're in for an entirely new experience.

Night fishing is indeed an adventure. It gives a new perspective to those of us who believe we know all there is to know about a stream. In fact, at no time are a stream's inherent mysteries and surprises more apparent than after dark.

Sometimes, you can hear them, see them, or even smell them, and they tantalize and intrigue you as if some ghostly apparition to which you can only vaguely and briefly relate.

On one of my first night trips to a bass stream, I stood knee-deep at the tail of a pool, casting a popper out into the open water before me. Before that evening, I must have fished this stream a dozen times during the day, taking only small bass. But for some reason, I stood convinced that the water held larger fish. On this night the moon was full, and its beam illuminated the middle of the stream and the open woods on either shoreline. It was almost like fishing at dawn, or just before dusk, as the moonlight transcended the landscape's dark blanket.

Along the shorelines, deeper into the pool, I could hear the commotion of fish hitting the surface and feeding beneath the overhanging brush. Although I couldn't see them, their disturbance on the surface revealed itself in the series of ripples pushing across the middle of the stream, spreading out, and then settling again before another fish would come up and hit a minnow. I cast the popper perhaps a half-dozen times before the first fish hit.

The smallmouth emerged from the water in a dark, elongated mass, engulfing my offering on the way up and pulling my line tight as it fell back. At once I was connected with one of the stream's nocturnal raiders, and I could tell that it was a decent-sized fish, for my reel's drag was speaking to me. As my vision was limited, I received most of my information from the feel transmitted through the rod and the sound of the fight. Four times the fish jumped from the water, shaking and thrashing, offering me brief glimpses of its glimmering silhouette. At one point during the fight, the fish danced on its tail from one side of the stream to the other before disappearing into the black space somewhere beneath the overhanging brush. All I could think about was keeping the creature away from the brush and logs next to the bank, but the fish had other ideas, which were revealed to me via the force against my rod and the flailing sounds on the surface.

At last I had the fish darting about my legs as I guided it in and grabbed its lower lip. When I hefted the smallmouth up high, where I could see its silhouette in the moonlight, my heart immediately resumed the pace it had assumed when the fish struck my popper. Its body was long, deep, and heavy. I removed the hook from its mouth and gauged its length next to my fly-rod. With my thumb marking the point high up on the rod's butt section, I released the fish into the water and felt the jetlike wash as it scooted away and disappeared.

When I returned home early the next morning, I took a tape measure and placed it next to the rod, anxious to see just how large of a fish I had caught. The thumbnail mark on the blank where the fish's lips had reached measured 18 inches! And thereafter, all I could think about was where that fish hides itself during the day.

My instincts had been accurate; the stream did hold some large bass. And my gamble of forsaking sleep for fishing time had paid off. But the experience had taught me so much more than the simple fact that nighttime fishing can be productive. It provided me with valuable insight about how bass behave in a small stream. I realized that these fish were completely synchronized to their environment, that they were masters of evasion and opportunity. I told you that I had fished the place a dozen times or so before my first nighttime adventure. And during those excursions, not once did I ever see one of these large fish. The results derived from those daytime outings would have had me believe that the stream held only small bass and pint-sized panfish, but I didn't fail to notice the ample wood and rock structure, the many weed

beds, and the variety of baitfish. I surmised that it was only a
matter of time before I encountered one of these brutes, and
after my night outing, I had discovered this magic time.

As is the case when fishing during daylight hours, you won't
always connect with a monster bass after dark. But your chances
increase dramatically. In those situations when you expect that
a certain stream holds large fish, which seem to vanish during
the day, a night trip may be just the ticket to finding them.

PREREQUISITES FOR THE NIGHT COURSE

Before you go out on a stream after dark, there are some things
you need to do in order to prepare yourself for this nocturnal
combat. The most important is for you to familiarize yourself
with your stream by fishing it during the day. The more you
have fished a stream in daylight, the better prepared you are
for fishing it after dark. And the less time you spend familiar-
izing yourself during those occasions when you can see, the
less prepared you are to fish at night. This is no different than
night fishing on a lake. If you go out on strange water after
dark, water you've never fished or scouted, you're simply
asking for trouble. You must find and recognize any potential
hazards, such as ledges, drop-offs, mud bogs, gravel bars, and
even flats. Noting the location of these areas is important not
only because they hold fish, but because they represent potential hazards after dark when you can't see them.

Another potential problem with night fishing, especially
during summer, is that this is the time when snakes are most
active. Snakes are found throughout the country and in most
of our good fishing spots. I've found that the areas that hold
the most snakes are those with slack water and plenty of wood
structure around the shorelines.

In the South we have to contend with the cottonmouth, or the water moccasin as it's frequently called. This snake is the subject of more tales and terror stories than perhaps any other. Many of these stories involve cottonmouths falling from overhanging tree limbs into boats, onto float tubes, and sometimes even onto anglers. I'm not an expert on snakes, but an internationally recognized herpetologist once informed me that water moccasins are acrophobic (afraid of heights) and thus aren't found in trees or overhanging limbs. I'm not implying that such an incident has never occurred, but I'm inclined to believe this man, who has handled thousands of venomous snakes (having been bitten only a handful of times, to which he attributes his lack of focus as the reason for these few accidents) over the years. Given that, I believe that harmless water snakes are often mistaken for the fabled cottonmouth.

However, if water moccasins are found in your area, you will occasionally encounter them while fishing a stream. You will notice them lying on mud banks, on or beside fallen logs, and atop beaver lodges or dams. Often, you will smell them before you ever see them, as the cottonmouth gives off a terrific stench. If you do encounter one, do not ever corner it. Rather, simply keep an eye on the snake and go the other way.

Ditto for any species of snake, venomous or otherwise.

Whatever you do, don't allow snakes to prevent you from fishing your favorite water, whether during daylight hours or after dark. Simply be aware of them, never crowd them, and pay attention to where you step and place your hands.

Fishing at night isn't an inherently dangerous activity, but it is sometimes beneficial to bring a buddy along, provided you blindfold him or her first to prevent them from discovering the path to your special fishing hole. If you are familiar with your stream, however, feel free to go it alone; just be sure to tell somebody where you're going and when you'll be back.

TACKLE FOR NIGHT FISHING

When you decide on taking a night trip to a small stream, remember that the bass's vision will be limited after dark. Therefore, you're going to have to concentrate on exploiting the fish's sense of sound and vibration. This is accomplished by using lures and flies that appeal to these senses. Some of the best conventional lures include rattling crankbaits and stickbaits, spinners, and buzzbaits. If the water is relatively clear, feel free to use sight baits, as the fish can see these, but only from a limited distance. This is why noise-emitting baits usually outperform those that appeal only to a fish's sight. If you do decide on sight baits, however, go with dark colors, such as black, brown, or red, as these provide more of a silhouette for the fish to target.

Unless your stream has an open canopy with few overhead obstructions, fly-fishing can be difficult after dark. The amount of overhanging brush, trees, and other shoreline obstacles present—along with your ability and comfort level—should influence your decision to use fly tackle, unless of course, that is all you use. When these potential hazards do exist, it is by no means impossible to use fly tackle, but you'll have to modify your casting in order to avoid snags. In the event you elect to use a fly-rod (and I highly recommend that you do), go with wakers, poppers, sliders, divers, weighted bunny leeches, and dark-colored streamer patterns.

LOCATION, LOCATION, LOCATION

By first scouting and fishing your stream during the day, you should have some idea as to where the fish will be after dark. This might be a certain flat, chute, run, or the shallow tail of

166   a pool. The magic area could also be a gravel bar, mud bank, grass bed, riffle area, or the plunge pool below a waterfall. Likely, it will be several of these areas, or even all of them, for darkness brings out the fish like a picnic does flies. Whatever you do, don't exclude an area simply because it lacks deep water. If large fish are present in your stream, then nighttime is exactly the time you'll find them in these areas. But you probably won't be able to see them.

NIGHT FISHING— THE LISTENING MAN'S GAME

Night fishing entails the use of your ears in order to locate fish, inasmuch as your vision is severely limited. This can be tough or even impossible in areas with swift, running water, but where you find calm water you can often find the fish simply by listening.

One night I was walking a stream bank next to a shallow flat. Several times I heard splashing noises upstream, just beside the bank. The moon was out in force, but all I could see was the shimmering water and the telltale sign of a feeding fish: ripples moving across the surface. Quietly, I moved upstream, and just as I did, the water next to me came alive, as a school of minnows leaped from the surface. Several of these minnows landed at my feet, sounding like rain as they pelted the mud bank in an effort to escape the sure death that was lurking only inches away. Then, movement in the water caught my eye, and I turned to see a magnificent swirl on the moonlit surface, 3 feet away and in water only inches deep. It was the kind of swirl that momentarily arrests your entire being, causing your jaw to drop and your eyes to bug. Like a toilet flushing, the water swirled, gurgled, and churned from the centrifugal force of a large predator fish (I guessed that it

was a bass, for I knew that this stream was loaded with them)
as it turned and moved off the shoreline.

That eye opener served to remind me of just how shallow an area a large bass will move into while hunting at night. For bass, a dark sky may be the most beneficial cover of all, and it changes everything.

Because of the fish's limited visibility, you can approach them much closer at night than during daylight. On nights with considerable moonlight, you'll still have to keep your silhouette in check, but the fish aren't nearly as spooky as they are in bright light. As is the case when fishing during daylight hours, the sounds you make are often what alert the fish to your presence. Thus, you have to be every bit as careful to avoid kicking rocks or logs and to move silently through the stream or along the banks. Just as the fish locate their prey by sound or vibrations, so too will they locate you if you're careless in your movements.

I've found that at night bass aren't as easily spooked by the sound of your lure falling into the water as they are during daylight hours. This is probably because they simply feel safer after dark. And although a quiet entry is always best, don't worry too much if your spinnerbait sounds like a bull inside a china cabinet when it hits the water. This certainly alerts the fish, but the subsequent sound and movement of your lure through the water will draw them in, because they have roughly located the position of your lure from the sound it made upon entry. And because bass are usually more active after dark, they show less reluctance to come and investigate. Sometimes the strike comes immediately after the lure enters the water.

Unless you're using a pure sight bait, you should be able to hear your lure rattling or popping as it approaches your rod's tip. In the water, you can be sure that this noise is transmitting even further and calling to the fish. Just as the bass home in on your bait by its sound or vibration, you too should be able to gauge the lure's progress or position by its sound; this is how you will have to track your lure. Later, as you get better at this game, you will acquire a feel for the lure, its position in the water, and its distance from the rod tip.

When fishing with conventional tackle at night, I like to use FireLine. There are many advantages to this type of line, including increased strength and abrasion resistance, and hair-trigger sensitivity. But another advantage is that it is noisy as it shoots through your guides on a cast. This doesn't alert the fish, but it tells me how far my lure is traveling through the dark air. Because I always fish a stream many times during daylight before ever setting foot in the water at night, I have a good idea as to its dimensions. I know the distance from bank to bank, the length of a pool or a run, and the location of isolated cover, such as logs or weed beds. Thus, at night, when I often can't see my target or my lure in the air, I can fairly well gauge the position of my lure in relation to the stream simply by listening to the sound of the FireLine. If the lure has shot through the air for two seconds (which would be revealed to me by the sound of the line slicing through the guides), traveling toward a stream bank that is 20 feet distant, I'll know that I need to stop my lure and get it in the water. Without this benefit, I would certainly put my lure on the bank or in the trees far more often.

Of course, this is all about knowing your equipment and the stream in which you're fishing, but I find that this line makes night fishing a bit easier.

Seasonal Availability

The hottest part of summer is certainly the single best time of the year to work a stream at night, but by no means are you limited to the warm months for this game. As strange as it sounds, winter can be a fabulous time to make a night move. Many times I have spent the entire day on the water with little or no success only to have confidence and adrenaline levels recharged after dark. Although the warmest part of a winter day passes several hours before dusk, the low light seems to trigger fish into a state of elevated activity. Such feeding activity is brief for a bass during winter, and it is important to note that not all of the fish in a stream are given to feeding at exactly the same time. Additionally, reaction strikes are much easier to solicit after dark simply because the fish feel more secure. Given this, night fishing during the winter can be extremely productive, provided you dress for the occasion and pay attention to what you're doing.

The aforementioned prerequisites apply doubly so to night fishing during winter.

Yet another excellent time to take to the water at night is during those occasions when, because of little or no rainfall, the water in your stream is unusually low and clear. Obviously, these conditions are synonymous with spooky fish, and sometimes, even extra-long leaders and camouflage clothing make little difference.

This makes night fishing a logical alternative. When the water conditions are such that the fish feel unnecessarily exposed, regardless of their position in the stream, then a dark sky becomes a crucial element to their activity and the genuine possibility of your success in catching them. The cover of darkness also reduces the chance that the fish will see you or your line.

Whenever you encounter this situation, you can be reasonably sure that the fish will be most active after dark.

MOVING ON

At night, don't spend too much time in one area. The fish are either there or they aren't. And if they are present and feeding, they'll hit your lure. Experiment and interchange your offerings and retrieves until you find what works best.

In order to help you get started, I'll list some typical areas within a stream and some of the baits that I have found effective in each.

Flats: Poppers; chuggers; divers; torpedoes; sliders; jigs; grubs; spinnerbaits; buzzbaits; crayfish imitations; shallow-running crankbaits; and dark-colored, broad-headed minnow imitations that are designed to push water (wakers, as they're sometimes called)

Chutes or runs: Spinnerbaits, shallow- and midrunning crankbaits, rattling stickbaits, pencil poppers, divers, dark-colored streamers, weighted bunny leeches, and jigs with large twin-tail trailers

Eddies: Dark-colored streamers, rattling crankbaits, spinnerbaits, jigs with large trailers, stickbaits, poppers, and dark-colored spoons

Pools: All varieties of crankbaits, spinnerbaits, buzzbaits, poppers, chuggers, divers, sliders, deer-hair streamers, marabou streamers, jigs with pork trailers, grubs, and large weighted bunny leeches

Riffles: Shallow and midrunning crankbaits, small- to medium-sized streamers, weighted bunny leeches, sculpin imitations, stickbaits, crayfish imitations, dark jigs with small trailers, and madtom imitations

Ledges: Spinnerbaits, shallow to midrunning crankbaits, stickbaits, leech imitations, jigs with pork trailers, spoons, soft-plastic tubes, and crayfish imitations

With any of these flies or lures, dark colors almost always perform best, because they provide more of a silhouette for the fish to target. However, don't overlook those lures or flies which incorporate flashy colors like gold, chartreuse, or yellow.

The thing to remember about night fishing is that you first need to do your homework by scouting and fishing your stream during daylight. Then it simply becomes a matter of putting in the time after dark. It may be later rather than sooner, but at some point you're a sure bet to get your eyes crossed when you hit the water at night.

Chapter 10

Small-Stream Secrets

ACH AND EVERY small stream, regardless of size
or location, has its secrets. By secrets, I'm referring in
some sense to surprises. Of course, after you're "surprised" for the nineteenth time, these enigmas are no longer
so enigmatic, nor are they regarded as surprises. But they remain a secret, known to relatively few—a few which now in-
cludes you, to some extent or another.

Some streams have secret locations, which hold more fish
than others. Some have secret fish species, which are relatively few in number, and still others have a secret time at
which they are best fished. The secrets I'm referring to, however, are a stream's largest residents.

Small streams don't divulge their secrets so easily. Inevitably, there is always a Lucky Joe who wanders down to the
bank and connects with a 20-inch smallmouth on the first
cast, but for the most part, these incidents are few and far between. A stream's secrets are only truly revealed after years of

fishing and scouting during all seasons, during all times of day or night, under all weather conditions, with all types of tackle and equipment, from all possible perspectives, with all possible presentations, and by all humanly possible means of holding one's mouth. In short, there are a myriad of variables, all of which have to be exercised with some degree of thoroughness before you can begin to truly understand a stream and learn its secrets.

The reason so few of us know a particular stream as intimately as our own living rooms—and thus so few of its secrets—is that the grass always appears greener on the other side of the fence. There are so many possible destinations to explore, so many opportunities, but so little time that we begin to think that we are cheating ourselves by restricting our favorite activity to a single venue. This is why those who know a particular stream best are, almost without exception, old-timers—those who have absorbed an environment for their entire lives. They differ so completely from the majority of us that, quite often, they appear lazy or even radical as they fish their favorite stream. But you can bet that these lazy, radical old anglers are fishing that way because over the years they've learned how to catch fish. They've learned what to do, what not to do, and seldom, if ever, do they leave the stream skunked. You could learn an infinite amount of angling wisdom and savvy simply by parking it on the stream bank and watching one of these old-timers in action. But you probably won't, because this book has convinced you to seek out those remote, overlooked, or maybe even inhospitable destinations, where you're not likely to encounter other anglers and where, by virtue of your stream's shallow water and miniature dimensions, large bass seem as unlikely to be found as woolly mammoths or saber-tooth tigers.

But I have a few secrets for you.

Because we've decided against sitting there on the bank, watching the old-timer cast a fly to elusive bass, let's assume that you're the salty dog, having spent the better part of your life fishing that stream.

As such, we've already deduced from your actions, old-timer, that you frequent the stream at all times of the day and night. It is apparent that you fish anytime you can, and each time you arrive at the stream, you wear a smile on your face. Why is this?

"Over the years," you explain, "I've learned that you can get the fish to bite at any time of day, at any time of night. Some days are better than others, but with your line and lure in the water, you always have a chance to catch a big fish. But,

Small streams harbor many surprises, such as this small-mouth/spotted bass hybrid.

176   you can't catch any fish if you don't go. So, I've learned to go fishing whenever I can. There is a direct correlation between catching big fish and time spent on the water. You can't have any consistency with one without the other."

We've also noticed another thing, old-timer. Your stream isn't exactly located in a remote mountain range. In fact, it's only fifteen minutes from a major metropolitan area, and state highways bisect this stream in three different places. Although it's not as busy as the nearby lakes, it does get a lot of traffic. How do you cope with this and still manage to catch fish?

"That makes no difference," you say. "The only thing that matters is whether the stream holds fish, which it does. And there are plenty of large ones out there. But these fish become accustomed to seeing anglers at certain times of the day. Mornings and evenings are popular, especially on weekends. I like to fish when there isn't anyone else around. If I arrive at the stream in the morning and discover another angler, I go to another area, or go home. The thing you have to do is fish at unusual times, when the fish don't expect to see you. This might be at noon, or at midnight. Put yourself on the water at a time when other anglers don't ordinarily fish."

That makes sense. But we've noticed your ability to catch large fish, even though this stream receives considerable pressure from other anglers. What's your trick?

"There are no tricks," you tell us. "You just have to be attentive. Notice what the other anglers are doing. What kind of tackle are they using? If you notice a lot of anglers using fly tackle, you're better off with a spinning or casting rod. Offer the fish something different, something that they aren't accustomed to seeing. I always try to be different from the others in the type of offerings I present."

And then you add: "And that goes for location, too. You see a lot of anglers fishing near the bridge, close to the highway. This is because it is so convenient. There are fish right here, and you don't have to go far to find them. But I catch most of my larger fish in parts of this stream where other anglers seldom go. I look for footprints on the bank, and if I find them, I go somewhere else. Sometimes, I may have to walk a mile or two, but I get away from everybody else."

That's fine. But what about those times when the stream is crawling with other anglers? What do you do when you can't get away from everyone else?

"Well, do you see that bank over there? The one with all the brush and trees next to the water?"

We do.

"Very few people ever approach the stream from that side. They almost always come in from the parking lot next to the highway. When I fish this area, I always approach the stream from that bank. I wear a camouflage jacket and cap, I crouch down and move slowly. And I present my lure from a different angle. The fish aren't used to seeing a lure swim toward this bank. It looks different to them, and maybe more natural. But like I said, if the stream is too crowded, I simply go home and wait for everyone to leave. Sometimes, I'll fish at night.

"And there's one other thing," you tell us. "Whenever fall rolls around, when everyone else is out in the woods hunting, I'm out here fishing, every day. The pressure is greatly reduced, and the fishing is quite good."

That's it?

"That's it. You just have to look for ways to be different. Differentiate yourself from the masses, and the fish will respond. Sometimes, it's easy to do, and other times, you have to walk 3 miles in the hot sun. But the fish will let you know when you're onto something unique."

We certainly appreciate your advice, old-timer. We'll be off now.

"Hold on," you say. "On your way out, why not swing around and cross the stream up here, and then fish the other side back to your car? That area never gets touched. Everyone else takes the easy way back. You might pick up a good fish or two."

And you might, if only you'll be unorthodox in your approach, if only you'll look for a way to be different from all the other anglers, or if you simply find a stream or a part of a stream that receives little or no pressure. In a few years' time, you'll begin to get an idea about your stream. And in a few more years, after fishing at different times of the day, in different seasons and with different tackle, you should have discovered a few of those secrets.

Now let's assume that you're new to a particular stream, a good-looking stream with ample cover, both deep and shallow water, and adequate forage. You feel confident that this stream holds some large fish, and you'd like to have a crack at them. Of course, there is no substitute for experience, no substitute for sheer time spent on the water. Nevertheless, you can accelerate your learning curve and improve your success ratio if you'll only read the water.

Applying what you already know about the features of a typical stream, let's jump ahead and concentrate on those areas where the largest fish are likely to be found. Our first stop is the largest, deepest pool in your stream.

POOLS

By now you realize that pools hold many fish, and the deeper they are and the more cover they contain, the more fish they hold. We've discussed how to approach and fish such a pool,

If you're looking for fish that will put your tackle to the test, pools are the place to go.

and how to thoroughly cover it. But we're looking for only the largest fish now, some of those elusive secrets. Where do we begin?

We begin by targeting the pool's major structural feature. This feature may be a boulder, rock pile, depression, log, dead-fall, brush pile, or something else. Of course, you know the location of this prime lie because you've spent some time scouting. But in the event that this feature is a log or brush pile, you may want to look again just to make sure it's still there. Streams that are subjected to heavy or particularly high water flow are likely to redecorate their interiors after heavy rainfall. High water displaces all but the heaviest objects and sweeps them downstream, where they lodge and hold until the next deluge picks them up and carries them even farther downstream.

Once you've determined that the main structural feature is still in place, then you begin your stalk, like a hunter.

Regardless of the time of day, expect a fish to be waiting when you cast your lure. A pool's main structural feature attracts and holds fish at any time of day or night. Smaller specimens may or may not be present, but you can bet that larger fish will almost always be on hand. These may not be the largest fish in your stream, but they very often are. In any event, you can almost count on taking a quality fish if you do everything else right.

Remember that your first cast is the most important. The first cast finds the fish in as natural a state as possible, before your successive barrage of presentations has a chance of alerting them. Also consider that at certain times of year, bass are extremely reluctant to come up to the surface to take a lure; however, they are subject to strike at any time of year if you put your lure right in front of them. To that end, go with a subsurface or even a bottom lure, one that you can place right in the fish's living room. This might be a streamer or a crayfish pattern, if you're using a fly-rod, with which you'll probably want to use a sinking-tip fly line. Or, if you're using conventional tackle, this might consist of a spinnerbait, crankbait, or a plastic worm, tube, or jig. Use something that mimics the natural forage found in your stream, and put it right in front of the fish. Use a slow presentation and the lightest line possible. And as always, keep your silhouette low and your movements to a minimum.

After targeting the pool's main structural feature, feel free to hit the head and tail if you wish. Keep in mind, however, that these areas are often more productive during periods of low light, and especially at night.

LEDGES

After—and only after—you fish the pool, find a ledge in the stream. The deeper the drop-off, the better. The best ledges are those that offer the fish overhead cover in the form of running water, washed-out rock, undercuts beneath logs, or a combination of these. Ledges provide bass with comfortable lies out of the current, and when running water is present overhead, they afford the fish a certain degree of protection from predators. But ledges are also prime ambushing positions, and bass know this. Very often, the largest bass in a stream will be found holding beside or beneath such a break on its down-current side.

The trick is simple. Approach the ledge from downstream, not too closely, and present the fish with a bottom-running lure. Cast upstream of your target, and give the lure time to descend to the desired depth before it reaches the ledge. It is important that your lure come into contact with the top of the ledge as it moves over. The resulting sound alerts the fish to what is ostensibly viewed as a crippled or easy forage item. It also helps you to track your lure's progress.

If you're using fly tackle, then by all means get a crayfish pattern tied to your leader (remember, the lightest line possible), provided, of course, that these crustaceans are found in your stream. It is frequently helpful to use a sinking-tip line and even additional weight in the form of split shot. Also, consider the size of your stream's typical crayfish, and use a pattern that is slightly larger. Don't worry that it may be too large, for it is quite likely that your stream harbors larger crayfish, which you simply haven't noticed. And large bass relish large crayfish.

This point was driven home to me one morning while fishing a small stream in Texas. On previous visits I had discovered a multitude of 3- and 4-inch crayfish and therefore used patterns of similar size. But as I fished the tail of a deep pool one morning, I noticed a peculiar object in the water on the stream bottom. It turned out to be a crayfish claw—a giant one. I fished it out and was bewildered by its size. The claw alone was nearly 3 inches, and I could only surmise that the size of the creature to which it had once been attached was probably 5 or 6 inches. I don't care where you live, a 6-inch crayfish is big-bass candy. From then on, I made it a point to use exceptionally large crayfish patterns and eventually found myself taking much larger bass.

Anglers who use conventional tackle when fishing ledges will find nothing so effective as the classic jig-and-pork tandem. Remember, use a *pork* trailer and not plastic. Don't use too large of a jig, or too small. Seldom do I ever use anything heavier than ¼ ounce when fishing small streams. In fact, I have found that a ⅛-ounce jig is perfect for most occasions, and when combined with a pork trailer, this little bait takes on a large profile and thus constitutes big-bass bait.

Cast upstream, work your lure to the ledge, and allow it to fall off. Once it falls, hold on!

PLUNGE POOLS

Plunge pools are those located beneath waterfalls. The force of the running water coming over the falls digs into the substrate and carves out a hole in the bottom, which is almost always deeper than the surrounding water. These areas concentrate bass for two reasons: food and cover. The current provides a constant supply of food, for which the bass barely have to move in order to eat, and the rushing water overhead makes for delightful cover. For these reasons, plunge pools often attract the largest bass in a stream.

We approach and fish plunge pools in the same manner as

ledges. This means approaching from downstream, using a heavy bottom lure and casting upstream. One exception, however, is when you're using a fly-rod.

Because plunge pools have a tendency to hold some of the largest fish within a stream, they can often be fished by casting a large streamer directly into the pool. As the surface here is already disturbed from the running water, there is no need to worry about a quiet or natural-looking entry. All you have to do is get a fly in the water—a fly that the fish can easily see—and they'll likely hit it.

For this trick I like a floating or intermediate line with a short, 3- to 4-foot leader. If the water beneath the falls is particularly deep, I'll even use a fast-sinking line. Go with abnormally large bait-fish imitations, in the size 2 to 1/0 variety, and cast these directly into the pool, below the falls. We're soliciting reaction strikes here, as the bass don't know where the fly came from. The bass think that the imitation has washed into the pool from upstream and, as it presents an easy and substantial meal, the offering warrants attention.

When using spinning tackle, I like a Texas-rigged tube of about 4 inches in length. Use a ¼- to ½ ounce weight in order to get it down fast and a 2/0 or so hook. Incidentally, the use of a wider-gap hook reduces the chances of a fish becoming gut-hooked.

If the tube makes it all the way to the bottom without being demolished, simply lift your rod tip and manipulate the lure with a slight jigging motion. If you get nothing with this method, then you're either placing the lure too far from the fish (which will correct itself with subsequent fan casts) or there are no fish present.

BENDS

Bends in the stream, especially the outside half of these bends, often attract fish because they hold deeper water. Such areas can be productive anytime, even during the middle of the day when it's hot and sunny. Add a log, some rocks, a boulder, or some other cover into the equation, and your opportunities at nabbing a large fish increase threefold.

Bends are also natural locations for eddies, seams, and sometimes ledges, which may or may not be visible from above the surface. Often, they harbor weeds or grass beds, log piles, and stumps, and may also feature nearby gravel or sandbars. And very frequently they mark a transition between one bottom composition to the next. Now are you beginning to understand why these areas can be so hot?

Some anglers like to approach bends from downstream, but I prefer to fish them across stream. I like to stand on the inside—or shallow—half of the bend and cast out to the deeper side. It has been my experience that quite often the best location on a bend is at the head, where the current is strongest, or in some cases just off the main current in an eddy, or below some overhanging brush beside the deep bank.

Bends lend themselves nicely to the fly-rod. I enjoy drifting large streamer patterns with the current, though occasionally I'll cast across stream, and simply retrieve it back against the flow. Baitfish-imitating patterns are a logical choice when targeting these areas, especially for the seams and eddies.

When opting for conventional tackle, you're likely to have success with a jerkbait or even a bottom-running crankbait. If you can locate the main channel, or ditch, that runs through the bend, work your lure down into this area and hold on.

Bends are also excellent early and late in the day, when

the bass frequently leave the deep water and move into the nearby shallows as they search for food.

TRANSITION AREAS

Generally, a small stream grows in depth and size from its headwaters to its lower reaches. The farther downstream from its source, the larger and deeper a stream becomes, until finally it reaches its confluence with another larger waterway. In most cases, these lower reaches tend to hold more and larger fish, though at certain times you can find lunkers lurking far upstream in surprisingly tight areas. As a rule, however, you can usually find some of the largest fish simply by locating transition zones along the stream. Look for those areas where deep water is confined, funneled, or surrounded on both sides by shallow water. This may be a secluded pool or an isolated bend or run. Larger fish typically take up residence in these areas, regardless of their location on a stream.

I regularly fish a small stream in Missouri's river hills, south of St. Louis. This stream holds good numbers of smallmouth and spotted bass, with many largemouth to boot. Formerly, I caught the smallmouth only in the stream's upper reaches, which is swift, rocky, and cool. The largemouth always came from downstream in the slower-moving stretches, which present a smooth bottom consisting primarily of mud with lots of wood structure and aquatic vegetation. The middle portions of the stream—which incorporate rocks and sand and which offer a moderate flow in both deep and shallow water—always gave up the spotted bass.

After many trips to this stream, I could predict what type of fish I was going to catch simply by considering the specific area in which I planned to fish. But that changed when I began fishing the stream in the dead of winter.

Isolated pools are typical holding areas for small-stream bass.

When the water dropped into the high 30s and low 40s, I began catching all three species from one specific location or another. Almost always, these locations were deep pools, and they were almost without exception located in the lower portion of the stream. Although each species has its preferred habitat and water temperature, when winter comes the fish do what they have to do in order to survive. And in a small stream, a bass's options are very limited.

Where I once took only largemouth from a deep, slow-moving pool, I was now catching smallies and Kentuckies. And the abundance of wood and lack of rock structure didn't seem to bother them. What I eventually noticed was that these few pools are deeper than most of the others on the stream, and many of them are located near spring outlets. Naturally, during winter, the water in these pools tends to run warmer than the surrounding water. I had located the fish's wintering quarters.

When fishing during winter, look to the deeper pools. Even though you may hit the water a dozen times or more and catch only small fish, you can be sure that if any larger specimens exist within your stream, they will be found in these deep-water sanctuaries. These areas offer the greatest respite from the cold, thereby attracting the fish, both large and small. And though the water may reach its warmest temperature sometime around midafternoon, don't believe that this is always the time when they're most active. During the coldest of winter conditions I've often had my best luck right at dusk, after the water had already dropped a few degrees from earlier in the day.

When the fish do decide to feed at this time of year (and not all of the fish will feed at the same time), they'll normally do so for only a brief time before shutting off once again. And during winter, a bass may eat only once each week, as its metabolism has slowed to the point that it needs only about a tenth of the food intake it does during the warmer months.

Obviously, the best lures for fishing during the colder months are those that lend themselves to the slowest of presentations. These include weedless jigs, outfitted, of course, with pork trailers. Lean toward smaller baits, and work them as slowly as possible. Frequent pauses are paramount to your success in winter. Drag the bait across the bottom, stop, pause, let it sit for as long as your patience allows, and then a little longer. When you do manipulate the lure, do so subtly.

At any rate, winter fishing is likely to be a slow proposition. This isn't always the case, but more often than not, you'll fish all day with only a couple of bites—if you're lucky. But at this time of year, these bites may come from some of the largest fish in the stream.

188   When you finally put it all together—the long hours, the odd times on the water, fishing under all perceivable weather conditions—and you begin bringing unusually large fish to net, you'll know what I mean about a stream's "secrets."

Chapter 11

A Year-Round Affair

SMALL BASS STREAMS offer many advantages to
the angler, but perhaps none more apparent and tan-
gible than their four-season availability. This is quite evident anytime you take to small water during the heat of
summer or on the coldest of winter days and then proceed to
catch fish. Such a feat can be difficult and time-consuming on
a lake or reservoir, for during these times bass concentrate in
select areas, usually on deep structure located well offshore.
For all but the most experienced anglers, locating and pat-
terning these withdrawn, big-water fish can be tedious and
frustrating. But small streams, by virtue of their reduced dimensions, concentrate their fish in relatively tight areas. So
finding them, and then presenting them with your flies or
lures, is much easier.

Because these stream bass are more accessible, they are
subject to taking your offering simply because you can reach
them. You don't have to eliminate hundreds or thousands of

acres of unproductive water, as is the case on lakes and reservoirs. Rather, you simply walk the stream banks and locate the likely areas. Once the fish are located, presenting them with your offering becomes an easy job. And because these bass are so easily accessed, your likelihood of success increases substantially, simply because the fish are seeing your lure.

Of course, this is to say nothing of spring and fall, times when the fish are likely to be found throughout the stream at every pool, flat, riffle, chute, run, and bend. These are some of the most productive and exciting times to fish small waters, as the fish are active and the weather conditions usually pleasant. Spring and fall are seasons that lend themselves well to the use of both fly and conventional tackle. They are the seasons for thirty-fish (or more) days. And while the crowds flock to the lakes and reservoirs, wreaking havoc on all that is precious to the angler, you can take some satisfaction in knowing that you'll likely spend the day alone at your secret fishing hole.

But don't allow these obvious advantages to make you complacent in your approach to fishing small streams. After all, bass are bass, whether they're found in a lake, bay, river, creek, or tiny brook. To that end, please realize that small-stream bass react to changes in the weather and the seasons just like those found in large water. These similarities grow more apparent when factors such as fishing pressure, time of day, barometric pressure, moon phase, water temperature, air temperature, pH, and water clarity are considered. However, the fish will react to these variables only as much as their habitat allows.

For large-water bass, this may amount to quite a lot. These fish have hundreds and often thousands of acres of water at their disposal. Should the July sun heat the surface temperature of a large lake to 85 degrees, the bass simply descend to cooler water, which may be found at 10 or 20 feet. Aside from the cooler temperature, the fish also benefit from the greater amounts of dissolved oxygen at these levels.

Yet, because of its restricted habitat, a small-stream bass is much more limited in its options. In a similar situation, such a fish would probably only be able to escape the warmer water by hugging the shadowed banks or holding in the deepest of pools or areas where springs empty into the stream. Any or all of the aforementioned environmental factors may send a lake-dwelling fish hundreds of yards or even several miles in search of metabolic equilibrium, but a stream bass's migration to the most opportune area available may encompass no more than 30 or 40 yards.

So, although the similarities of large- and small-water fish are quite apparent, the habits of the latter are almost always carried out on a much smaller scale.

THE ACCESSIBILITY OF SMALL-STREAM BASS

When water temperatures plunge into the low 50s, then the 40s, and maybe even the 30s during winter, bass seek the warmest water available. In a lake, this warmer water may be located 30 or 40 feet below the surface, or even deeper. But in a small stream, the bass are limited to much shallower water, perhaps only 5 or 6 feet overall. Consequently, they are much more accessible to the angler.

Similarly, during summer, when surface temperatures reach 80 degrees Fahrenheit or more, lake and reservoir bass move down to the cooler, more oxygenated water and are often found suspended just above the thermocline. But do you think that the bass of small streams are able to find such a haven? They are, but it won't be nearly as deep. Summer tends to concentrate fish below waterfalls and riffles in well-oxygenated areas, which are often no more than 4 feet or so in depth. As you might have guessed, these fish, too, are more accessible to the angler.

And then there's spring and fall. During these times, the fish are scattered all over the stream. Because of the warmer water temperatures, which spur the bass's metabolic rates upward, they feed aggressively. You can find these active fish in a lake or reservoir, but you'll probably have to work for them, covering miles of shoreline and running down a trolling-motor battery or two. But in small water, you can frequently keep busy all day by working a half-mile stretch of your stream. Again, small-stream fish are highly concentrated and thus are more easily accessible to the angler.

By now, you've noticed many similarities between small- and large-water fish. Both are subjected to a variety of environmental factors, any or all of which can instigate behavioral changes in the fish. The hot, sunny weather warms the water, and the lake-dwelling fish move deep. Ditto for small-stream bass. Once again, the difference is that the fish found in the latter destinations are limited in how far they can go. Bass in a small stream may winter in an area no more than 100 yards from that where they spend the warmer months. Yet, in a large body of water, this variance may be emphasized in miles.

On the other hand, fish in some small streams travel much greater distances, often leaving one stream and moving into another. In fact, smallmouth bass in certain Minnesota and Wisconsin rivers have been known to travel 100 miles or more in transitioning from their summer to winter waters. But we're dealing with small creeks and streams here, so it is important to note that if your stream possesses those characteristics necessary for sustaining good populations of black bass, then you'll probably find them in that stream all year long. And if you'll only invest the time to learn about your stream, its fish will be highly accessible to you, the angler, at any time of year.

Now let's examine a hypothetical small stream and find out where you're most likely to encounter black bass during spring, summer, fall, and winter.

SPRING

In early spring, male bass move up into shallow areas with sand or gravel bottoms and begin fanning nests. The larger females eventually move into a nearby transition area in anticipation of spawning. They hold just outside of the shallow water where, at the first sign of unfavorable weather and continued cold water, they can easily move back into deep water. But in early spring, when water temperatures begin rising consistently, they'll eventually move up to the nests and spawn. At this time of year, bass—and especially the largemouth—may be found in extremely shallow water. These spawning areas are often located next to weedy or grassy banks, usually in areas that are highly exposed to the sun.

Thus, at this time of year, we often find bass frequenting flats and other shallow areas. But the largest fish will invariably occupy those shallow areas with deep water nearby. The reason deep water is so crucial to spawning bass is that it provides the fish with safety. It is true that you can find many, many spawning bass on a shallow flat or shelf, far from deep water. But if you'll look closer, you'll notice that these are almost always fair-to-middlin'-sized fish. The largest bass always spawn in a shallow area where there is a nearby cut, ledge, or drop-off, and deep water. The largest bass get to be that way by being wary, and being wary means having safety no more than the flip of a tail away.

If your stream features backwater areas, these can also be

good. Another excellent area in which to locate spawning bass is near a bend in the stream; along any place that offers a shallow shelf, bar, or ledge bordered by deep water; and just off the main current. If such an area features a sandy or gravelly bottom, then it can be even better.

Once the fish are on the beds and spawning, they can be difficult to catch. In fact, they'll often only escort your lure out of the area, without striking. But if you catch them before they get into the act, you'll find yourself into some of the best action of the year. Usually, this is the time when you'll catch the largest fish, which are the egg-laden females. Anytime you are fortunate enough to catch one of these sows before the spawn, please remember to handle the fish gently and promptly return it to the water so that it may fulfill its biological obligation.

In the event that you stoop so low as to keep one of these fish, remember that you're taking not just a single fish from the stream—you're taking hundreds and thousands of possible fish in the form of eggs. And keep in mind that the removal of a single mature female bass from a small stream can later have exponentially large and adverse consequences.

By April and May in the South, and later in the North, weeds, grasses, and other aquatic vegetation will begin to rebound from their winter dormancy. As such, they begin giving off oxygen and offering good cover for all manner of insects, crustaceans, amphibians, and fish, both large and small. Naturally, areas with any sort of aquatic growth are likely to hold bass and should be covered thoroughly. The key word, however, is "growth." During late fall and winter, when the vegetation dies, it pulls oxygen from the water. Having just the reverse effect, the fish will steer clear of these oxygen-deprived areas at such times.

The good thing about spring is that you'll find fish all over the stream. What's more is that they're active throughout the day, from morning to evening and sometimes throughout the

night. This is perhaps the single best time of the year to catch
a large fish in shallow water. Before the spawn, the fish are
eager to stuff themselves because they instinctively know that
once on the beds, feeding takes a back seat to spawning. For a
few weeks afterward, the bass will usually be noncommittal
and the fishing spotty. Give it a little time, however, and once
they realize that they're famished from their recent propoga-
tional activities, the feeding lamp will once again light up.

Keep in mind that smallmouth and spotted bass prefer to
spawn in deeper water than the largemouth. Look for gravel
or rubble bottoms either within or adjacent to deep water.
Some of the best locations are those behind boulders, logs, or
ledges, where the fish are protected from the current. Again,
deeper areas possessing these features are usually best for the
smallmouth and spotted bass.

By the time the spawn has ended, the fish, although they
will remain dispersed throughout the stream, will be gravi-
tating towards a summer pattern and should be highly active
and willing to strike at your flies or lures.

SUMMER

During summer, the fish are often found throughout a stream,
but they'll hold in those areas that meet their needs for food
and shelter. But because summer's temperatures often warm
many streams to 80 degrees Fahrenheit or more, the amount
of dissolved oxygen the water contains will also determine
where you find the fish. Largemouth bass can tolerate warmer
and slower-moving water, but the spotted bass and especially
the smallmouth prefer cleaner, cooler, and swifter water. To
that end, when it gets really hot, look to those areas that provide highly oxygenated water. This means locations with at
least a moderate current. Some of the best include mouths of

Lightweight fly rods rigged with floating lines and streamer flies are perfect for use during summer, when water conditions are often low and clear.

feeder creeks or other tributaries, springs, riffles, and waterfalls. These areas are better for smallmouth and spotted bass, but you may also encounter a largemouth from time to time.

Another perennial summertime favorite is the pool. Pools hold fish at any time of year, but during summer you may find the bass "stacked up" in these deep-water havens. If you fish early and late in the day, the pool tails can be very productive, though when the sun is high in the sky, concentrate on the head (which should be well oxygenated) and main body, near any structure.

Perhaps the most important cover for bass during the summer months is shade. I have learned that shaded areas hold fish at any time of day, regardless of the depth of the water that they shade. Of course, the best shaded areas are those in deep water, such as pools and runs, but wherever you find shade, even if it's located on a shallow flat, fish it hard. And should you find a shaded area that contains abundant weeds or other aquatic growth, fish it even harder, even if the water is only inches deep. When fishing on summer days, shade is the name of the game. In fact, you'll almost always find that these spots produce best when you most wish that you had a piece of shade overhead.

Chutes and runs are another solid bet for summertime bass. Anytime you encounter one of these features, especially during the warmer months, cover it from one end to the other. Another logical lie is the outside and deeper half of a bend. If this area is shaded, look out.

Above all, look for those areas that offer deeper water, shade, and a moving current, then key on them.

FALL

Fall is my favorite time to fish, anywhere. Because there are so many sportsmen and -women who equate cooler temperatures and briefer periods of daylight with hunting, the fishing is often phenomenal simply because the crowds are absent and the fish less pressured. Another reason fall can be so good is the fish instinctively sense the approach of winter. Falling water temperature, the decreasing intensity and length of daylight, and the arrival of cold fronts all serve to trigger bass into action.

In my part of the country, on the southern plains, fall is the most delightful time of year. Unfortunately, it is also the briefest. In early fall, the fish are typically reluctant to desert their summertime patterns, though with the arrival of the first cold fronts they get the message. And things change in the blink of an eye. The fish go from lethargic to highly active almost overnight, but before you know it, they've moved off to their winter quarters.

In short, if you have the opportunity to fish during fall, take advantage of it. Because it won't last.

When fishing a small stream at this time of year, of course you should target pools and runs, but don't overlook flats, riffles, or other shallow areas. Later into the season, the action will often be best during the middle of the day, when temperatures are at their peak. You can often use this to your advantage by taking a leisurely breakfast and arriving at the stream about midmorning or so. By the time the action heats up, you've been in the water for about an hour, and you too are on form, ready to go. You can also use this warm-up time to scout other areas of your stream in order to get an idea of where the fish will be at certain times of the year.

Late in the season you'll often find bass holding along the shoreline in shallow, sun-exposed areas during the middle of the day. As a rule, shallow fish are usually active fish, so they're prime targets. If you're fishing early or late in the day, target deep areas, which are likely to hold inactive fish and more of

Large smallmouth are often caught during late autumn, on overcast days, when the action is otherwise slow.

them. These fish, too, may be caught, but you'll probably have to use subtle, finesse presentations.

WINTER

During winter, you can catch fish in shallow water, though the window through which you'll have to work in order to do so is very small and elusive. Most of the time, however, you'll have to look for the deep pools where the fish are more likely to hold. Slow, subtle presentations are mandatory for these fish, though the most productive time of day will vary according to current moon phases and other factors. During winter, afternoons and evenings will frequently prove better than mornings for the simple fact that the water has a chance to warm a few degrees throughout the course of a day. And if you think that during winter a 2- or 3-degree increase in water temperature isn't significant, then think again. In winter, this is just about all you have, so don't misplace this knowledge.

Late in the season you can begin looking at the shallow, sun-exposed flats. Fish will often move into these warmer areas during February and March (or later in the North) in anticipation of spawning. The best areas are almost always those that are highly exposed to the sun for as long as possible which are also located near deep water.

If you discover the location of any springs in your stream, then mark them for future reference. Springs emit a continuous water supply that bears a consistent temperature. In many areas of the country, this water will run from the mid- to high 50s. This water is cooler than the surrounding water during summer and warmer than adjacent water during winter, making springs good areas to fish during these times of year. If you locate a spring in or near deep water, then rest assured that you have found a honey hole for summer and winter fishing.

During winter, best results are often obtained by working deeper water with bottom lures and flies.

These areas can often be located simply by carrying along a stream thermometer and using it to take frequent readings.

If summer fishing is about shade and the water's oxygen content, then early winter is a game of water temperature (in late winter, water temperature isn't nearly as important as the length of the days). In fact, you can often throw out all other variables and tailor your act solely around the time when the water reaches its warmest temperature. This is particularly true during early and midwinter. Although this isn't always a sure bet, it affords you the greatest possibility of success. But when the old man seems like he's running out of cold, frosty breath, you need to be out on the water. Spring is certainly the time for large fish, but the largest bass in a small stream are never more likely to be caught than during late winter.

Chapter 12

The Vulnerability of Small Streams and How to Protect Them

*I*F I WERE TO DROP the name of Stream A on Monday, Friday would find it overrun, overfished, and no longer overlooked. This is why I haven't named any of the streams I've mentioned in this book. Small streams simply can't handle this type of popularity— any popularity. Therefore, it would behoove you to take some ownership of your home waters. Do your best to protect them and preserve their integrity.

Most of the small, remote, and unknown bass streams that I've visited support remarkably healthy and productive fisheries—at least at this writing. In the majority of these cases, their successful fisheries were due in large part to the streams' inconvenient, secretive, and often inhospitable locations. Although it is true that many strong bass streams are found within minutes of major metropolitan areas, the best are almost always located far from such centers of technology, development, and convenience. To put it another way, people and small streams don't mix. Our objectives and quest for so-called "progress" and "quality living" are entirely incongruous with the raw innocence of a small waterway. Therefore, it is absolutely imperative that we minimize our impact on these tiny jewels, for their value is worth far more than the richest king's gold.

We start by practicing *catch-and-release* fishing.

This term has become a buzzword among the trendy, elitists, purists, traditionalists, informed, as well as the not-so-well informed who want to appear as such in order to impress their friends or fellow club anglers. But this isn't just a politically infused term that has somehow fallen into our conformist vocabularies. It is both a physical practice and mentality: One stresses that you consistently release the fish you catch, and the other demands that you keep the fish's best interest at the forefront of your mind. This involves anything and everything related to the fish's well-being. Some of the actions commensurate with a catch-and-release philosophy include playing a hooked fish quickly and using sufficient-sized tackle with which to bring in and land the creature in an efficient manner, thereby minimizing lactic acid buildup and mortality. Additionally, limiting the fish's time out of the water, as well as reviving it before release, are equally as important.

Yet another thing we can do to minimize our impact on the fish is debarbing our hooks. The benefits of barbless hooks include easier penetration and release, which benefits both fish and angler. Many anglers would argue that barbless hooks lose fish, but I would suggest that poor hook sets and allowing slack into one's line during the fight (as well as improperly seated knots and using old or frayed line) are the primary reasons fish are lost, all of which may be classified as angler errors.

While this practice and its inherent methods are necessary to sustaining healthy fish populations in many, if not

Gentle handling, reviving, and releasing the fish we catch are absolutely essential if future generations are to enjoy fishing for bass in small streams.

most, of our nation's lakes, reservoirs, and rivers, they are absolutely imperative for small bass streams. Failure to practice catch-and-release fishing on such a diminutive waterway can strip the stream not only of its fishery, but of its very integrity and identity, thus disrupting the entire ecosystem.

Because small-stream bass are more confined, exposed, and accessible to the angler, they are also more easily pressured and overharvested than their large-water cousins. The removal of even a few mature female bass from a small creek can have quite adverse consequences in succeeding years. The natural, functioning equilibrium of many of these small streams is so easily disturbed that a single irresponsible angler, over the course of a few hours, can ruin the stream for fishing for years to come.

Please note that I harbor no aversion to keeping a few fish for dinner from time to time. In fact, I much prefer fresh fish to beef, pork, or poultry. But when you're looking to fill a stringer for the table, you should look to the stocked and state-managed lakes and reservoirs, or at least the larger rivers. Small streams should not be viewed as grocery stores. Whenever I decide to bring home a few fish, I'll almost always target the larger lakes in my area for crappie, walleye, or catfish. I no longer eat black bass. Over the years of chasing after these fish, learning about them, catching them, and frequently eating them, I have developed a deep respect for my quarry. Of course, I feel that black bass—whether largemouth, small-mouth, or spotted—are certainly too valuable to be caught only once. The only exception to this, at least as far as I am concerned, is with overpopulated farm ponds or lakes, where unregulated fish populations often exceed a habitat's carrying capacity. Farm ponds are particularly prone to overcrowding and, therefore frequently harbor massive populations of stunted fish. In these instances, the removal of a certain percentage of these fish is beneficial to the health and well-being of the entire fishery.

At any rate, treat small streams as if they're natural museums, which in many ways they are. You wouldn't be allowed to bring home any of the exhibits for dinner or for any other reason. So practice catch-and-release, and watch the collection boom. The resulting benefits take many different trajectories, but don't think that they will miss the curator, which is you, dear angler.

In the North, acid rain and other industrial runoff have been the demise of many small streams. In the South, we have to contend with litter. I don't know why the folks up north seem to realize the importance of putting trash in its place, whereas those down south continue to miss or ignore this fundamental characteristic of normal, sane, and functional human society. Even early North Americans, living 10,000 years ago, had designated areas to which were relegated waste and other refuse. But in our modern, highly efficient, and complex world, which is the United States during the twenty-first century, there remain a few of us who can't seem to find the time, the gumption, or the moral or ethical aptitude to properly dispose of our garbage. I'm not implying that those north of the Mason-Dixon Line are perfect, but we southerners are facing a real problem with this issue.

To begin with, litter just looks bad. It degrades the environment and, when found in the very areas where we pursue our hobbies, passions, and interests, it causes all outdoorsmen and -women to appear as irresponsible savages. Theoretically, each of us is a steward of the particular environment in which we pursue our life, but ridiculously few of us want to punch in on the clock and assume our shift. Or worse, we are paralyzed by fear or apathy whenever we witness another degrade our planet by littering, which causes us to look the other way and tolerate this fraud of humanity.

However, until we find the collective wherewithal to not only confront and punish these violators, but also to organize and sustain legitimate campaigns to preserve our natural playgrounds, we are doomed to wallow in our own swill. There will always be those who, because of bankruptcies of character, tolerate or participate in such nonsense. But it is up to the majority, the responsible and dedicated contingent of society, to police the scum among us. It is up to us to expose them and disallow their individual and collective assaults on our lives and environment.

208   In order to keep what is precious to us and to preserve what is left of our world's natural integrity and our precious small-stream fisheries, we must fight the good fight against litterbugs and any other goon who thinks that he or she can degrade our environment without consequence. Failure to do so will surely result in substandard fisheries and fewer and fewer venues where we can pursue our hobbies and passions.

But the streams aren't all we have to protect. Riparian areas—those that abut the stream banks and that are often wooded—are equally as important. Riparian areas are small ecosystems unto themselves, including a myriad of trees, plants, animals, and other life. These areas are vital to a healthy stream, and one of the most important functions they serve is to prevent soil erosion. Despite this, riparian areas along many of our nation's small waterways are in jeopardy because of urban sprawl, suburban development, mining, livestock overgrazing, and the like.

Thus, it stands to reason that in order to protect our small streams, we must also defend the adjoining riparian areas. We can go a long way toward that end by supporting organizations that promote habitat preservation, advocate the fencing out of livestock from riparian areas, and fervently defend our natural resources from degradation caused by immoral and unethical developers and other rapists of the land.

And inasmuch as we all live downstream, runoff, whether private or industrial, has to be stopped. To that end, we must support those individuals and organizations whose promise and intent it is to protect our natural resources. Furthermore, we must punish those responsible for such blatant acts of runoff by boycotting their products and refusing their services. Unless we grow backbones and stand up to these bullies, future devastation of our small streams seems unavoidable.

Therefore, it is up to us to police ourselves. We must take

some ownership in our small bass streams—and indeed all of our natural waterways—and treat them as the priceless, irreplaceable jewels they are. Above all, enjoy them. Ask yourself, what about your individual stream do you most enjoy? Then work to ensure that that aspect is protected, insured, and secured each and every time you pay a visit. The beneficiaries of this special policy are our succeeding generations.

INDEX